The Romance of the Faery Melusine

Also by Gareth Knight on Skylight Press:

Experience of the Inner Worlds
A History of White Magic
The Magical World of the Inklings
Yours Very Truly [collected letters]
To the Heart of the Rainbow [fiction]

Forthcoming:
I Called it Magic [autobiography]
Faery Loves and Faery Lais

The Romance of the Faery Melusine

ANDRÉ LEBEY

TRANSLATED BY
GARETH KNIGHT

SKYLIGHT PRESS

First published in Great Britain in 2011 by Skylight Press,
210 Brooklyn Road, Cheltenham, Glos GL51 8EA

Designed and typeset by Rebsie Fairholm

Illustrations taken from a number of late 15th century woodcut prints, except
for those on pages 137 and 151, reproduced from *Histoire de la Maison Royale
de Lusignan* by Pascal (1896).

Printed and bound in Great Britain by Lightning Source, Milton Keynes

www.skylightpress.co.uk

ISBN 978-1-908011-32-9

Contents

André Lebey (1877-1938) is a forgotten man in French literature, although he was an associate of well known figures such as Paul Valéry and his circle.

A man of parts, he was a Socialist deputy during the 1st World War and a popular writer and speaker on Freemasonry. He showed his great love for ancient tradition in his historical/legendary works *Le Roman de la Mélusine* and *L'Initiation de Vercingétorix*, published in the mid 1920s. They were highly popular in their day, but have since been neglected, and he himself regarded as too much of an enthusiast, lacking academic rigour. However, to my mind this is one of his great strengths and a misunderstanding of what he was trying to do. He makes the legend of the Faery Melusine more vividly alive than any scholarly rendition, whilst his imaginative treatment is close in content to the original romance recorded by Jean d'Arras in 1393.

I have to say that André Lebey is not an easy author to translate. His vocabulary is vast and, in his love for medieval imagery, full of terms from ancient heraldry, hunting, costume, armour, delicacies of the table, and flora and fauna, some of which defy every dictionary possessed by me, including those in Middle and Old French. And on occasion, like Balzac in *Contes Droliques*, he likes to venture into a semblance of medieval French of his own devising, in addition to fragments of poems in Latin or in Occitan. Thus there are points where I have been forced into a little guesswork and paraphrase. But if I have fallen short, I console myself with the thought that if something is worth doing it is worth doing badly.

Above all I have endeavoured to maintain the vibrant spirit of the original, and to make the faery Melusine a loveable and lively presence no longer confined to the Francophone world. After all she may have founded the family, town and castle of Lusignan but she originally hailed from Scotland where her faery mother was queen!

Gareth Knight

·I·

The Great Old Hunter

ur story begins with a great hunter of long ago, now legendary, none other than Aimery, Count of Poitiers.

They lived close to nature in those days, even in towns. Fields came right up to the walls and the forest was close by. In hamlets and villages wild animals in their lairs could watch unseen all that went on around human dwellings. Foxes and wolves knew just when to raid. God help any child left playing on the doorstep, forgotten of an evening. On winter nights, in times of famine, packs ran through the streets, howling under the cold moon. Arrows, stones or spears were useless against them, as their numbers lent ferocity to their hunger during the night, and only the first light of dawn saw them depart.

They came down in a sudden rush. The peasants sighed and townsmen huddled for comfort against their wives in their warm beds as they heard the scampering of clawed feet on the paving stones. In narrow alleys where the houses leaned against each other, with bowed windows and gable ends overlapping or set back like monks' cowls, the passing of the dense pack, cheek by jowl, brushed the walls, iron studded oak doors, bars of lower windows with their leaded panes, to make a strange rustling sound which seemed somehow diabolic. Any who heard them pass and raised the oiled paper of a window flap to see the last go by, crossed themselves, consigning them to the Devil. A strange wild smell, something like sulphur, hung in the frozen air, stinging the nostrils, as in a room where a fire, smoking before going out, has left a scorched smell like He of the cloven hoof.

The forest stretched beyond, menacing and dangerous, full of the unknown, concealing the surprising and the supernatural. Great wildcats like small tigers abounded there, and when they prowled into lordly parks might leave with a white or multicoloured peacock, its cries choked within their maws of gleaming teeth. Between the lines of fir trees on the heights, bears licked with long tongues the honey from the nests of bees, which splashed in drops of golden liquid down their white or grey fur. All along the bushes by the pathways the eyes of lynxes burned, watching the old women, bowed under loads of kindling. Children who followed claimed to see stars at the tips of their tufted ears.

From a juniper thicket in a gully of the Rhine in the Black Forest, Charlemagne had once seen an old auroch of the Gauls, the European bison, emerge; and had not the fair warrior Hildegarde, daughter of Hildebrand the good Duke of Souabia, not put all her weight on the lance by which she pinned his leg to the ground, her father's guest would have been dragged by the beast, disembowelled, into the forest. The charcoal burners crossed themselves when they spoke of the raucous lowing of the great lone beasts that roved through the woods.

Yet all through the land, evil reigned only if heroes failed to confront its dangers. It seemed that the one existed to give rise to the other, for humans do not show their mettle if left to themselves.

In the forest of Broceliande in the heart of Blue Brittany, in the talons of a hawk on a golden perch, the Code of Love was to be found. Bound in crimson leaves, it held the bold and tender rules that guide knights and noble ladies through all the delicate stages of exquisite favours up to the great joy of shared passion. But a minstrel will later sing for us about that.

In those days men identified with things that could lead them further into the unknown; they sought in all directions the extension of their physical and spiritual power. So they believed and so they lived, sure of themselves and strong at one moment, at the next deflated and weak, falling to their knees for restoration from another source, the Lord Jesus Christ.

And things, animals or people, trees or weapons, were more themselves. Man developed without dissociating or abstracting himself from the world. In short, he knew how to love it, to give and to take in many ways, as he needed. And the law of God prevailed over all.

Hunting, so different from our own, more justifiable because more difficult and necessary, maintained the extension of human power. Under the protection of St. Hubert it was held sacred. The complex rules of venery and falconry detailed its elements. None knew them better than Count Aimery. Everyone said this who knew him. How to train a pack of hounds, to leash the dogs, assemble them, set them off; to fly or moult a bird, to hood it, offer it the lure and the glove, be it wild falcon or peregrine.

In deep gorges or wide plains, in forest or river, he always knew what best to do. Not content only with lords of the air, sparrow hawks and falcons with the speed of barbed arrows, he had dogs of all kinds, spaniels, bratchets, terriers, great danes to hunt his lands, even Tartary hounds like those of St. Louis, whose breed resisted rabies.

In aerial hunting his wings quested everywhere as his servants beat on drums to make the prey rise. He ruled the fate of all creatures on his land including the birds of the air. To enter a wood, search it, raise a stag, sound a horn, were things that ever gave him pleasure.

Although he strictly preserved his rights, he was just and good and never cruel. Not like the Bishop of Auxerre, Lord of Inteville, who crucified one of his guards for having stolen a few merlins. On the other hand, perhaps he would have been like a certain Saracen prince, as told in the chronicle of Eleanor of Aquitaine, who, when a great hearted falcon attacked a royal eagle and, helped by two others, brought it down at the feet of all the court, had it immediately put to death. Because, he said, it had been an act of treason to attack its natural superior.

Taming birds of prey pleased the Count of Poitiers. Fine proud heraldic and handsome, noble rulers of the sky, he made obedient and faithful like dogs. He saw a masterpiece of the will in this conquest of tireless wings and powerful steel-like talons, which flying high beyond the range of the human voice would, at a sign, a gesture of the hand, return to table or cage. For the falconer moulded his instruments to his desire, recomposed eye and feather, transformed habit and instinct, as if by enchantment. From the summits of wild rocks he plucked the autours, the falcons, and used them as he chose.

And what is finer than a hunt of this kind when women take part? Everywhere *en fête* without and within, when hearts beat faster in beasts and men. All colours shimmering in fabric and in feather, in the gold of gems and the steel of arms. The pretty distraction of a long evening, flowering like a rose on the cheeks of a châtelaine, as a bird rests on her tendered glove, docile to her gentle voice, as is sung in the Lay of the Golden Land:

> *She sang a lay so beautiful and sweet*
> *That birds who came to hear her song*
> *Soon after sang it too.*

The eyes of some beautiful fair ones are blue but there are others of a golden brown, like their hair, and warmer. Whose eyes, wide open, great and singular, are the best rulers of a bird, which cannot pull away when those eyes are affixed to its own. They are magnetic, like those attributed by the poet Homer to Juno, the wife of Jupiter.

It can only be marvelled how a bird, be it sparrow hawk or gerfalcon, rustles all its feathers on a female glove – with rayed ruff embroidered with fine pearls – as the lady looks at him and speaks to him. He is beautiful himself, with crested hood of silk and a silver bell. A greyhound, standing by the horse, becomes jealous, raises its long head and with a furtive look bares its teeth, then jumps, despite itself, when she launches the falcon into the light wind and calls to it. Finally turning its head in disgust when the bird returns with prey intact, neither dead nor even wounded.

Ladies like to fly them against the grain-eaters of the plain; quail, partridge, wood pigeon, as well as thrush, bustard and doves, but Aimery liked above all to contend with herons, storks, even swans, curlews with their long plaintive cry, wild geese and water-birds of wide wingspan whose wiles and courageous defence increased the drama of combat. He never tired of seeing them gloriously cut the wind. His gerfalcons, goshawks and sparrow hawks were always of great enterprise, all well mewed, lively and vigorous. Aimery would not tolerate a bird with feathers in disorder or broken quills. He had them painstakingly and minutely prepared.

The roads of France in those days were travelled by wandering bird catchers with hawks of all kinds for sale. The great falconer levied a tax on them, but they met with great welcome at his castle in Poitiers where they sold rare birds, such as those employed by Saracens against the ibis, ostrich or gazelle. But the rarest, the most powerful, were the white falcons of the north, like those that Bajazet demanded for the ransom of Jean de Nevers.

Townsmen, imitating the lords, possessed some fine hunters on the perch, and girls of modest upbringing even equalled the châtelaines in dressing a fine crested bird on the glove. It was the simple daughter of a tradesman of Chalus in Champagne, a good and beautiful maiden, who gave to Gerard de Nevers the famous hawk hooded with fine gold surmounted with a glowing ruby, that was so well disposed that it took all birds, however small they might be, without harming them in any way. One day, it even brought to Gerard a skylark that carried round its neck an annulet of love.

A curious thing, if quite natural, that all occupied with birds will know, is that with them the law of the sexes is reversed; the females big, strong, majestic, used mainly by men; the males small, capricious, fantastic, more difficult to prepare, but which women prefer. They like male hawks, lanners, sacers and merlins, not only for giving good service but for being less tiring on the wrist.

Count Aimery also liked to hunt the deer, roebuck and the stag, especially the stag, whose flesh comforts the sick, and whose hide, smooth to the touch and supple, covers great manuscripts under wooden panels with a velvety greenish-yellow fur that never splits. What is more, it is sacred flesh, and the excellent monks of St. Denis use it to make shrouds for the kings of France.

These are like the stags that Aeneas killed with arrows and ravenously ate after his shipwreck on the African shores of Queen Dido, who built

Carthage. Nor let us forget the rarest of all, the white stag, whose pursuit and capture was always marked by prodigious events. All knew that the knight whose blade brought down the rare beast had the right to choose the most beautiful from all the maidens ranged about and kiss her on the mouth. This was often the cause of duels, as happened in the full court of King Arthur at Cardigan on the edge of the famous Broceliande, despite the advice of Merlin.

However, above all it was the boar which tempted and tested the count. It seemed to him that in killing one he achieved a work of piety. The black beast, charged with execrations, was in his eyes the symbolic figure of the Antichrist.

When one of his hunters arrived to announce the presence of an enormous boar in the woods of Colombier, he decided without further ado that next day they would leave to hunt it at dawn.

·II·

The Boar Hunt

There is great delight at the start of a hunt in the morning. It seems as if all is at one with the dawning day, bringing new adventures yet unknown. Everything sings, as if to say nature is awakening – from the clink of the fine coats of mail and small arms and the conversation of the knights, to the cracking of whips and shouts of the huntsmen round the pack of baying hounds. Then, with the neighing of a horse it seems that all comes together, setting afoot the fate of those who set forth and those whom they hunt.

The sun cuts through the mist to make sparkling reflections, lighting up the gaudy colours of the riders. For on a hunt, as in war, perhaps even more so, the lords and knights, counts and barons, put on their finery – ablaze with scallop shells and stars, vivid and distinct images each on its coloured field. It seems as if all the world is here, famous lords, their vassals and guests, bare headed or wearing hunting caps. And as their horses have no headpieces or silken robes, they wear their insignia, the emblems of their fiefs and lineage, on their chests, embroidered on the cloth or painted on leather doublets. Here are wings, alerions, eagles, hydras, salamanders, and tarasques, moons, crescents and towers, serpents, leopards and wolves, crosses, shells and stars, all emblems of nobility and spirit, fixed for ever, like a hieratic form of writing. A little in the fashion of an ancient people whose first teaching was by drawing, as in ancient Egypt.

From dexter to sinister, from chef to point, divided per pale, per fess, per bend, per barre or by further partition into three, or four or six or yet again in up to thirty two quarters, in gold, silver, scarlet, azure, green, purple or black, with billets, lozenges, diamonds, triangles, squares, with lines wavy, indented, embattled, engrailed, or nebuly, and charged with emblems too numerous to mention and all under crest, helm, and mantling, it would be tedious to describe the arms of all present. So we give just those of Count Aimery, which were of azure with a golden wren and golden sun on one half of the shield, and on the other a black eagle soaring on a silver field. Thus all brought with them and about themselves, emblems of their domains, their castles and their ancestors.

Through the crowd of valets and huntsmen went his nephew, a tall young man, handsome, graceful, intelligent, skilful in all things, ready for anything; called Raymondin, with sword at his side and spear hung from his neck. He rode his horse so well with his legs that the reins seemed merely for ornament, as if cut from a picture in a missal. Whenever a quarry was raised he would be to the fore, behind the dogs or among them, leading the hunt, galloping fast.

Now he increased his pace as an enormous dark monster, trampling all before it, was plainly seen – for it was merely the end of the month of the Ram, the forest still bare and not yet green. In a narrow clearing, where no doubt the boar felt it was in too much open space, it turned suddenly on the leading dogs, so quickly that four were gored, two greyhounds, a mastiff and a great dane. Then it plunged back into the thick wood, to zigzag now to the right, now to the left, diverse and unpredictable, so they might easily have lost it.

More than five times, on a wide path or at a crossing, it turned about again with such force and fury that neither dogs nor hunters nor spearmen round about could pen it in. All this brought about, little by little, a feeling of doubt, far removed from how they had felt at the start. And they saw too that their master, always so keen, was likewise concerned.

The beast seemed to sense this, and rushed here and there, returning to renew the game as if it defied them all, with its glistening white tusks bloodied red, and its great black mass. More than thirty dogs lay stretched out, torn open, to mark its way.

"It is the very Devil himself," groaned a baron.

"What do you mean?" cried Aimery, furious and heated by the chase, unable to stifle his rage. "Will you let the son of a sow scare you! Get after it!"

The hunt began again, this time with the Count of Poitiers at its head, the rest panting along behind. But when the monster turned again, Aimery missed it, and was carried past by his horse. Then Raymondin, leaping from his own, sword in hand, took the lead, and although hampered by a dog, stabbed it in the neck.

The boar, as if it had felt nothing, retreated a little as Raymondin prepared himself to meet its charge. But the beast seemed content with knocking him over without trying to trample or gore him. Then it turned on its tracks and took off in another direction, as with a sudden twist of its loins it threw into the air a dog that had tried to leap on its back.

The hunt now seemed to take on the air of a *danse macabre*, and all who followed it, whether pale, or flushed and sweating, looked like wild men, their clothes awry and torn, dejected, distraught, deranged, like horsemen of the Apocalypse. The whole forest seemed blighted, as if harrowed by phantoms. The raucous sounds of the horns, the strident screech of the trumpets, the deeper sounding brass, increased the impression of hell. Even the dogs seemed transformed, with their matted hair, hollow flanks, crazed uneasy running, apprehensive, pitifully howling, slobbering tongues hanging from their jaws.

The wind when driven by storm breaks no more branches or boughs than the black boar, except that it brought down only those in its solitary way. Nothing could stop it. From time to time it repeated its trick of suddenly turning on the following bratchets, greyhounds and great danes, now more cautious of it, waiting for the kill. Each time it showed itself more savage and more speedy. The horses, covered in foam, hair matted, drenched with sweat, nostrils bloody, tongues hanging out, refused to obey their riders, rearing up or falling. Many valets and squires no longer followed. Few lords were still there. No one persisted wholeheartedly.

As the light declined in the darkening woods, the beast, seemingly diabolic, increased its vigour. There remained only a few distracted dogs, ready to die in a last cause, but soon they were either stretched out on the ground or cowering, howling at the death of those that no longer moved.

As the shadows lengthened, only Count Aimery and his nephew kept up the infernal chase, Raymondin above all. But he sensed his uncle, little by little, was falling further behind as the boar went on ever more strongly. Desperately torn between a desire to hold on till the end, however dangerous, but yet not abandon his master, he could not decide what to do.

Finally he heard his voice, from far off, call out to him: "Good nephew, the Devil keep it! Leave off this cursed hunt. And cursed be he who set us on that hellish beast!"

Raymondin still hesitated. Although the boar had almost escaped, he could perhaps still follow its trail, keeping an equal distance between it and the lord of Poitiers. But now it was almost night. Darkness descended on the forest, and through the extended branches of the trees with their close-packed budding leaves, the sky appeared only at moments, revealing neither moon nor stars to help the two lost hunters.

A voice, as if lost, small and confused, called indistinctly – "Raymondin!" He stopped. The sound of the distant boar, hardly perceptible now, died away, and all was silent. Then a horse approached at a canter. Raymondin waited, feeling rivulets of cold sweat coursing down his body under his clothes. His horse pushed through the fine wet foliage as he advanced slowly in the direction of the Count, to a clearing bordered with thick undergrowth which seemed a good place to stop. The sky could be seen more clearly here.

Soon Count Aimery appeared. He who had always borne himself so upright was now bowed over, his face troubled and drawn.

"Dear nephew," he sighed, as if overcome by weariness, "let us wait here until the moon rises. It is hardly possible to go on and certainly unwise."

"As you please sir."

Raymondin dismounted and began to collect branches, which he piled up, and with his tinderbox lit a fire to which the horses and both men drew near. All four began to feel warmer as the moon appeared, a slender crescent that seemed strangely close. The pale light of its beams rendered the expanse of sky more blue all round. The stars appeared quite quickly, precise as if they had always been there, clear, sharp, so vibrant that the angles of their alignments seemed somehow malefic.

Then came the hooting of an owl close by, as if the bird of silent flight was an emissary from beyond the grave, its call played on a flute made from the bones of the dead who lay in their sepulchres. For some time neither Raymondin or the Count spoke. After a last cry the ill omened bird passed by, swooping low over Aimery's horse, before it disappeared. Then, far off, its cry was repeated three times.

Finally it ceased and the two men and the horses breathed again, while the Count, who had bent his head under the baleful flight looked up again at the stars. Aimery could read their unseen affinities, and a deep silence enfolded the two men. That of the forest, mysterious, sometimes troubled, overlaid with something else, pertaining to the sky, infinite, absolute, inexpressible.

The Count was an expert in astronomy, which included the occult. He could read the stars of the celestial planisphere almost as easily as a manuscript. The good people of Poitiers were a little scared to see him pass nights on the great tower of his castle surrounded by strange instruments in the form of spheres, mirrors and compasses, in the company of an astrologer named Arbatel, a stranger from the East with its strange gods. The more curious who crept as close as possible to the platform suspected that the sorcerer made his pupil drink the juice of mandrake bark to confuse and then to dominate him. They averred that while working with the astrolabe and crosstree their master addressed him with deference as "Father", like a priest, when not conversing incomprehensibly in an unknown tongue.

Standing before Raymondin, his head a little tilted back, with his white beard and grave and noble features he appeared like some kind of priest king. His nephew, who loved and admired him, remarked on the increasingly reflective expression on his pale face, at first sad, then serene and at peace. He sighed and let his head fall back. Looking straight ahead of him fixedly with half closed eyes, as if into the impenetrable thickness of the forest and his destiny, he murmured:

"Oh God who art the master of us all, such as we are. Lord of the universe, your creation is infinite, your work admirable, your ways incomprehensible. I thank you for having taught me to read the grimoire of that great sea above, ploughed by thousands and thousands of ships of gold. The vulgar may call them stars; they know not that they are, some brilliant, others dim, the reflection of human lives. When a star falls, a ship disappears from the infinite. Our destinies are written above."

Raymondin was worried and surprised.

"Leave off your dreams, sir. It is not right for so high a prince, whose realm is so magnificent and vast, to let your heart be consumed and led astray by uncertain dreams of necromancers. It is ridiculous, dear lord – for this earth is so much your own, so good, so solid, under your feet."

The Count gave a distant smile, imperceptible but knowing, superior to fortune.

"Fool! Happy fool! You do not know your own joy! If you could see up there the extraordinary riches and astonishing adventures written there for you, you would be amazed. But believe me, you will see it come to pass very soon."

The youngster thought neither good nor bad of that, but was curious. Who would not be when it is a question that concerns their own fate?

"In faith, dear sir, tell me what you see above. Since you are convinced my future is so fine, I would be only too happy to know. Perhaps you are right after all, and there are things hidden there that we should know."

"By God, then you shall know, young sir! And it would be better for you to profit from what I say. I am an old man, and have enough friends and vassals. As for you, I love you more than any other, and want great honour to come your way. I tell you, that in this very moment that we speak, if a subject were to put his lord to death, he would soon become the most powerful and honoured man that ever was! Not only that, from him would come a noble line, known and remembered until the end of the world…"

"I would find that hard to believe from anyone but you sir, whoever it might be. But from you, in the faith of a squire and a vassal I accept what you say as true, if it is something you would have me believe."

He had hardly spoken when in the bushes close by came the sound of breaking brushwood as if a wild animal was passing through. Aimery and Raymondin seized their swords and placed themselves before the fire, facing the bushes from whence the noise of snapping branches came.

And only just in time. An enormous boar appeared, like the one they had just lost, massive, aggressive and baring its teeth.

"My lord," cried Raymondin, "Quickly! Climb a tree! You are tired. Leave me the honour of dealing with the beast. It will not take long."

"God forbid, nephew, that I should abandon you in such a fight!"

The bushes were thick through which the beast struggled, so it could not rush out upon them at once, only its terrible snout protruding. Raymondin, seeing its neck exposed with its feet still entangled, advanced and struck with his sword but hardly wounded it. It only became more furious, and tore its way free. Disregarding the young man, it charged with all its force straight at the Count and knocked him flying. Dropping his sword, Raymondin seized a spear to drive into the side of the beast. The spear was thrust with such force, for in the sudden danger he had the strength of ten, that it not only passed through the hairy flank of the boar but struck the old Count as well, pinning him to the ground, so gravely wounded that man and beast, one on top of the other, died together.

What passed through Raymondin's heart at the sight of what he had done can hardly be described. He thought his pounding heart would break. He rolled rather than lifted the animal to one side and leaned over his uncle, his tears dropping onto the wound he had made, and wept as he had never wept before, as one lost, as indeed he was.

"Ah Fortune," he moaned, before the body of his uncle, whom he had always adored. "Perverse, insidious Fortune, why have you done this to me? Why make me the killer of the one who loved me best? Where am I to fly? I dare not think what will become of me! From now on, all who see me, or hear of me, will view me with contempt. They will judge me deserving of a shameful death, as the vilest of sinners. To think that my lord said that I would be the most honoured of my line! Hollow dreams, lies, for that secret science never revealed to him his sudden danger; neither that nor the owl's cry that I forgot as quickly as it came. Alas! He deceived himself and deceived me in good faith. I will be the most dishonoured of men, that is what all will say. So now I must fly from here, find a life elsewhere, and perhaps, please God, make amends for my involuntary crime!"

He saw the Count's horse nuzzle its master's body and that of the boar, and then look at him with great round eyes. Then his own horse did the same, and the two beasts looked at one another with a fearful questioning air.

He seized his own steed, leaped upon its back, and spurred it into a wild gallop he knew not where, even faster than he had ridden in the hunt. This time as if he were being hunted himself by someone or something unseen. Desperate to escape, he felt no other wish than to meet with sudden death, perhaps at a sudden blow, smashed against a tree.

Thus, all but bereft of his senses, he rode madly through the forest into the night.

·III·

The Faery at the Fountain

About midnight Raymondin saw a fountain that he recognised, for he had often passed by. It was called the Fountain of Thirst, although some called it the Faery Fountain. Women spinning by the hearth fire on winter evenings told stories about it, like threads of gold spun from their distaffs, sparkling through the fatigue of their work.

The fountain was at the head of a pleasant oval lake as seductive as the stories to which it gave rise. The place seemed made for cool water and stories in much the same way that the stories evoked such enchanting waters and their surroundings. Anything seemed possible here. The beauty of the place had a presence that became more vivid the more one gazed upon it.

Despite himself, too broken to have any pressing need for the unknown, Raymondin gave himself up to it, and through his eyes something entered from beyond himself. Reflected in the mirror-like waters, hardly disturbed by a light breeze, a great rock, solid at the base but divided at the top, rose like the image of a dark and mysterious castle. Beyond the lake a meadow appeared golden in the pale light of the moon, drawing his gaze to quest into the far distance for things that could not be seen. To right and left rose the forest, tall, massive, full of shadows, unfathomable too, if in a different way from the plain. Under the vague light neither revealed its secrets any more than the far horizon.

The landscape near to him was clearer under the moon, but in so far that it defined things better, his first impressions left him and his fears came flooding back. The fatal spear had not only pierced the boar and the Count, it had transfixed his heart. He felt it there as a pang of remorse. It would always be there wherever he went, heavy as a gravestone, barring him forever from peace of mind.

However, rising more brightly than that of forest, rock, plain or fountain was his own reflection, shimmering at the edge of the pool, that descended to mysterious depths where ancient fish, pale with age, could be seen clear under the pure and magical twinkling of the starlight. Raymondin wished he could stay. To be helped in some way by these things to forget the sorrow that lay so heavily upon him.

Failing that, why not sleep? He let his heavy eyelids droop as if he were going to sleep. For a few seconds he even lost consciousness, and his weary horse, which divined the state of its master as he sat more heavily in the saddle, proceeded to a walk.

Now three white ladies, standing still until now, began to dance on the grass before the Fountain. One of them seemed to be their leader, for the others copied her movements in great sweeping curves. She leaped lightly, the veils of her sleeves rising around her, accompanied by her two followers. They turned so quickly at the moment Raymondin passed by that his horse, suddenly aroused, took fright, shied, and set off at a trot.

"By my faith, he who just passed looked like a gentleman but did not act like one! Making no greeting when he met fine ladies!"

She spoke as if she did not know the rider, for she did not want the other two maidens to know that she did, nor what she intended.

Then she added: "As he said not a word in passing us by, I shall go after him!" And she ran as rapidly as the goddess Artemis, and stopped his horse with her hand on its bridle.

"Sir vassal," she said, her voice sweeter than the sweetest song, "from where do you get this great pride, or even rudeness, to go past three ladies without saluting them as you should?"

Half asleep and half in dream, Raymondin said nothing, and did not even touch his cap. Did he hear her? Only he knows, the story teller thinks not, for he remained silent as if he had ceased to exist, until she said in a louder voice:

"Why, sir dawdler, are you so disdainful as not to answer?"

As he remained silent she seized his hand and pulled.

"Good sir, are you really asleep?"

He must have been, for starting like someone suddenly awakened, he grabbed for his sword, thinking the Count's men were upon him.

"Sir knight," cried the maiden with a silvery laugh, "who are you going to fight, and with what? Do you take *me* for your enemy?"

Suddenly coming to himself at the sound of her melodious voice, he opened his heavy eyes, and before such beauty smiling upon him in the milky light, now so bright that it seemed like another day, another world, he wondered if he were still alive. Realising that indeed he was, he leaped from his horse. Standing before the maiden, whom he saw was as real as himself, he was filled with wonder and bowed low before her.

"Lady, pardon my unintended discourtesy. I lay my apologies at your feet, more numerous than the drops of falling dew that, reflecting you, take on the aspect of pearls. By the faith of my mouth and my heart, that do not lie, I was possessed, body and soul, by a dark affair that grieves me cruelly."

She stood before him, seemingly transparent, as if her flesh shone with the force of light. She gazed at him. He gazed at her, and was transported by her beauty.

"I believe you willingly," she said. "But where are you going at such an hour? Don't be afraid. You can tell me. If you have lost your way I can guide you. There is no path in this forest that I do not know."

He lowered his eyes and sighed.

"I thank you lady, I lost my way and have been riding through these woods all day since dawn. And to tell the truth I hardly know where I am."

Seeing he lacked faith in her and would not admit what it was that tormented him, she took it upon herself to say, "By God, Raymondin, do not try to hide from me the reason for your pain. That is quite useless, for I know it as well as you."

Too stupefied to know what to reply, he remained silent, overcome with anguish that his secret was known. Baffled by the recent events that had come upon him, and also perhaps a little bewildered to find himself not too unhappy that this being before him was aware of things that, up to now, he was sure had been known to no one.

"My good friend Raymondin," she murmured, as if it gave her pleasure to repeat his name, "I am the one who, next to God, can help you best to gain wealth and honour in this mortal life."

Dumbfounded to hear the same words that he recalled the Count of Poitiers saying, bound by sensations and obscure feelings that he had neither the strength nor the courage to explain, he listened with growing surprise and yet relaxing contentment.

"I know that against your feelings and intentions you have killed your uncle and your lord. You were flying because of that, thinking yourself a criminal, when I met you. Do not be afraid that I know all about you. And do not suppose that this knowledge came to me by evil ways. I am as faithful a Christian as you are. But Fate, for all that, is Fate. We can only control a part of it by our actions or the consequences that come from them. We have to take what is offered when it is to our advantage. Without me, without my counsel, you cannot escape being accused of murder when the Count of Poitiers was killed. On the other hand, if you listen to me, and take account of what I say, I promise to make you the greatest lord of your line and the wealthiest."

The words of Aimery came back to him now with particular force. He found them almost exactly the same as those that had just been said to him. Lifting his head, he saw the same sky, the same stars which held the prophecy of his fate twinkling as if to reassure him of the invincibility of their teaching, which passed the understanding of men and put a seal of truth upon the words of the old lord. All this pressed upon him, powerfully, crushing. The way of Fate and its laws and the perils that threatened him, of which the least were exile and death. In any case his honour was lost for lack of proof, even if he were thought to be innocent. Time pressed. He had to make up his mind, come what may.

And so he decided.

"Lady, even though I do not know you," he replied humbly, "I thank you for your promise and accept your kindness. I will do whatever you ask, if it is possible, and what a good Christian can do with honour."

"That comes from a pure heart! Have no fear, I will never ask anything of you that is against your religion or mine. But that is not all – I have another request to make of you, so listen carefully."

Her light blue eyes, flecked with grey, that in the moonlight seemed like mother of pearl, held him with a penetrating gaze that had an air of promised happiness.

Was he going to be the victim of an illusion, or of an increasingly unforeseeable reality? She no longer looked at him dispassionately, while he, in return, found her delectable. In the warmth of her presence he no longer felt so tired or so desolate. He began to feel a man again, full of vigour. Something new had come upon him that was almost like desire as he realised how beautiful she was.

"Before going further," she murmured as if responding to his secret thoughts, "you must promise not only to take me as your wife, but never again to doubt – you understand, *never*, sir knight – that I would conduct myself honestly and in a Christian manner, beyond any sorcery."

Impassively, she waited in the quiet night, crystal clear, in which he could hear his heart beating, and then that of the lady. He was not surprised at first, that it responded to his, like an echo. For they had drawn together without being conscious of the fact, and he observed the rise and fall of her breast under her corsage, that seemed to him like a promised land. From her beautiful breast his gaze descended. Why not? Was it not done for every lady to show herself desirable? All the more reason for one who wanted all, including marriage and yet further sworn promises.

What went on in the very depths of his being, where the essential intimacy resides? On this point again, only he knew, and she, who knew all. She went on to the oath with firm grave voice, and even though he knew her not at all, he so much wanted her.

"Lady, I will loyally do all that I can. I accept you for wife, before God and in the face of ourselves, and will marry you as soon as you wish in a church."

She replied as if she knew that all had been for ever decreed and would now come to pass.

"That is well, dear Raymondin, but there is something else."

Surprised, he could not stop himself from blurting out "You have me at your mercy!"

"Not at my mercy, but at ours, above all, our mutual joy. May it last always, for ever. If I promise you all happiness so as to be happy myself, do you blame me?"

"Certainly not!"

"Then hear my request. It is that you must swear by all the sacraments you hold holy as a Christian that on each Saturday, from sundown till dawn on the following day, never – and I will say it again so there is no doubt about it – never must you try to see me in any way whatever, nor seek to know where I am."

Could he retreat, having come so far? It would have been to lose her, and she seemed even more beautiful to him, sweet and attainable. The promised happiness to which he looked forward concerned him less than she herself, whom he wanted to know more and more, and above all to possess. What minstrel can describe the irresistible power of feminine beauty when it gets under a man's skin? None can, and that is no doubt how things will remain till the end of the world.

The murderer of Count Aimery was conscious now only of his desire. His former sadness, his remorse, even his exhaustion he threw off in exasperation. Finally, to absolve himself of the slightest doubt that might arise from far down within him, he told himself that if he did not consent he would be lacking in gallantry.

He thus agreed solemnly to all.

"On my life, I swear that never on that evening or that night will I do anything that might be to your detriment, and that I will, in all goodwill and honour, seek to know nothing about your absence."

"That is good. I believe you," she said in her turn, in a tone in which joy was not untinged by melancholy. She said no more for a while, as, embarrassed a little by their mutual tenderness and the link established between them, they hesitated to hold hands. She was the first to risk it, and after a glance behind toward her companions, now discretely out of sight, she drew him to sit at the edge of the lake on a great stone which formed a seat against the trunk of a tall lone pine.

"It is a matter for you now," she said, "and for you alone. So listen carefully."

After a pause, she explained to him what he must do concerning the death of the Count of Poitiers and advised him to say nothing about it. She detailed the attitude he should take toward the children of the deceased, the young Count Bertrand and daughter Blanche. She went into further great detail that he promised to follow to the end, without fail. If some of this was inclined towards deception he did not notice but followed her willingly.

She smiled with satisfied grace, certain that he would be true to her from now on, and ended by giving him two little wands that she appeared to pull from the tree:

"Dear friend, I give you these two wands, whose stones have special virtue. The first, which has haematite, preserves from accidental death by weapons. The second, which contains carnelian and chrysolite, gives victory in any dispute or combat. Carry them with you always and you will evermore go safely."

He twirled the two little sticks, and they shone in the night with the different stones set into the wood. Nothing now surprised him. Nonetheless, feeling him not yet entirely confident in her, she added, looking up at the stars:

"The virtues hidden in the stones are set there by the order of Nature and the Stars under the will of God. Have faith. The spirit, humour, blood and soul that rules them is also influenced by what we imagine, and the stones do the rest. They correspond to the four elements of which they are made: water, air, fire and earth. Then by the slow mysterious process by which they were made, a resolution of earth in their particles and a condensation of very pure water, their existence is precipitated, in which nothing can ever change. You wear upon you talismans of the Sun, and of the Orient, where it shines with greatest strength."

He listened to her as if to a living poem, and by the first light of dawn realised that she was, for him, the most beautiful precious stone in the world, as she loosened her hair so the oval of her face was framed like a gem in its gold. Then she began to comb it, and as he admired the fine silky, deep and long tresses he saw the wooden comb that ran through them had carved upon it a beautiful naked woman also combing her hair. He wondered if this might be herself perhaps, and smiled to himself, which she noticed and interpreted well. She left the comb in her hair, where it stayed, and grasping his hand, with the other drew him to her.

He bent his head to her breast where her heart was beating firmly, sweet and strong, then raising his kisses the length of her neck, and then to her chin, he met her lips, to which she responded with great joy, for he felt them soon part. Thus they exchanged their first kiss, which we leave to themselves, and thus they remained for some time.

She was the first to break away – it was always she, indeed, who led – and in a soft voice that she forced to render resolute, she said,

"Go now, so you can return to me the more quickly to tell me what you have done."

He wanted to stay, and said so, but she insisted.

"Time presses, and it is for your own good. If you stay longer your absence will be suspect. I do not want to lose you, my sweet friend, now that I have found you."

While he collected his horse she carried her left hand to the comb, and the other languorously stroked the stone in the place that was still warm from where Raymondin had been sitting. When he returned to hold her a little longer in his arms, he held back at first the better to admire her face, encompassed by her fair hair. But as her eyes were also filled with him, neither one nor the other could drag themselves apart.

"How I love you!" she sighed, almost in a whisper.

She rose and held out the stirrup for him.

"But it is for this that we must part."

Then when he had mounted, her head leaning against his leg, she said, laughing: "You won't forget me?"

He laughed in turn.

"You won't go back on your word?"

"No!"

Then suddenly he realised he did not know her name, and asked her.

Then as if the voice he heard came from the infinity of night and the forest, played on an enchanted harp like those of the bard kings of ancient Ireland, he heard:

"*Melusine…*"

·IV·
Granting the Charter

alloping through the trees away from the fatal hunt, the young lover realised his fate had taken a similar change of direction. His horse too, happy to return, increased its pace as the faint light of dawn began to bathe the forest. It was midway through March and the damp and cold encouraged speed. The pace of their passing tore down the last dead leaves resting here and there on the lower branches, whilst in Raymondin's ears beat rhythmically the name that had become the most beautiful in his life. Like Siegfried after he had killed the dragon, when the bird song began to awaken he believed he could understand it – and that it celebrated Melusine.

M e l u s i n e !

The unique meeting at which he had spontaneously committed his faith had added a baptism of love to his rebirth. Even his sadness faded on recalling the moving words, so soon proved to be true, of the noble count whose body lay under that of the black boar. And a high noble line the grand old man had foretold under the trees.

From the edge of the wood of Colombiers, the beautiful town of Poitiers could be seen, rising in solid tiers above its long stout walls, dominated by the strong castle with its crenellated and machicolated defences one above the other. Catapults and mangonels alternating with archery slits in unified lines between high narrow windows, sparkling with lead encompassed glass. The whole city appeared of an ochre colour from afar, the same tone as its stones. Above the tumble of sloping roofs of brown or red tile or slate, jostling in disorder one upon the other, the narrow tower of the keep bore at its masthead the lord's pennant, a stamen of scarlet and blue undulating almost transparently in the light air, that was suddenly lowered and then raised again to half mast.

Almost immediately, a bell whose chime he recognised, the Catherine, the heaviest in the cathedral, slowly sounded the knell, six times. After a short silence, others responded, one after the other, from the bell tower of every church, like the falling of distant crystals of hail. Then those of the convents of three villages and a suburb close by replied all together, the great bronze bells seeding with sound all who heard them in the neighbouring lands – informing the furthest away, one by one, who knew nothing as yet – of the mourning for the most high and powerful lord Aimery, count of Poitiers, of Liguge, of Nouaille, of Augles sur Auglise and other places.

His long shafted spurs with widely cut rowels pressing less against the flanks of his horse, Raymondin came to the thatched huts with beaten earth walls of red clay, surrounded by thorn hedges, scattered round the plain at the foot of the city ramparts. Now he began to hear cries of lamentation. At the postern gate that stood before the draw bridge over the ditch, he found he had arrived just after the body of the count. He shivered at such a coincidence, for there also was borne the massive body of the diabolic beast from whence all the trouble had come. Following its victim and preceding their double murderer.

"Weep! Weep!" lamented the men who carried them, as the people ran towards them. "Weep! Weep! This son of a sow, they say, has killed our good lord!"

Everyone, stupefied, looked on with eyes full of tears, while others cried: "Cursed be whoever called that hunt! Curses on whoever started it!"

Their grief was general and sincere. Their affliction extreme. Raymondin lost no time in robing himself in black. Far from Melusine, his grief returned, pressing and tormenting. Fortunately, he also thought of what she had promised, and recalled her counsel, which stopped him from speaking out, as several times the feeling mounted within him to admit his fault courageously and make public penitence for it.

He thus shared genuine tears with those of the countess, of her children Bertrand and Blanche, and with all the court, comforting them with the thought that, whilst suffering unbearable misfortune the soul may feel itself alone against the unknown, at the same time it may feel that only a small part of things is represented by passing earthly reality, and whilst realising its powerlessness may cross the divide between hope and resignation.

While they prepared the church of Notre Dame the Great, whose pure Romanesque lines facilitated the display of armorial banners, Raymondin gazed from the square over the surrounding horizon – for Poitiers is built on a rounded plateau. He viewed with sadness all these lands, fields, parks, valleys and hillocks, and forest with hidden lakes, from whence Count Aimery raised tribute, foraged as he chose, pursued the game of flesh or feather, whose life was held sacred to all – apart from lords, their dogs and their falcons.

Soon he saw the men arrive who carried the boar on a great hurdle, followed by a crowd of people trailing branches, hurling threats and curses at the monster. Arriving at the centre of the place, they put the beast to the ground, while the frenzied people piled up branches, which was soon accomplished, the crowd being many. Six burly woodsmen, long haired and unkempt, with resinous torches held aloft, stood around it like heralds at arms. Then the boar was solemnly hoisted up by the strongest of the woodsmen, inclining their torches to set the pyre on fire, which with a frightful stench burned on into the night.

The next day, when the count's magnificent funeral took place, the ashes, some still warm, were thrown to the four winds by those who could not find a place in Notre Dame the Great during the service, despite its three naves. Through the open doors came the voice of organ and choir. Yellow wax candles of great size, like hundreds of stars, were carried to the four cardinal points to mark the fate that had befallen the city of the Pictaves. Stone saints from the porches, their fingers raised in blessing, were carried with their insignia. St Denis at the head, St Andrew with his short cross, St Martin with his tunic, St Lawrence with his grill, St Joseph with his square, all those that I forget, the Holy Virgin with her Child, the Good Shepherd with his lamb, all, as far as the cherubs with their little heads in their little wings. Also, Mary Magdalene and Martha, St Ursula, St Radegonde, St Cecilia, and St Bridget – recently brought from Brittany.

Alas, all was soon gone. Time demands necessity and order. Memory, less alive, finds its room too full of shadow, half opens the shutters and then the window to the sun, turns the key in the lock and opens the door, until one day all is forgotten. It needs to be so for life to be possible. Thus grief leaves the human heart, even the most wounded, apart from rare exceptions, of which the truest perhaps are those of which nobody is told. Who could weep forever, and not accept that some things can no longer be, ever, whatever one does? Reeds bend against the strongest wind and then spring back, or they break. The children of the earth are a little like reeds along the river bank, or in the middle of its course in the torrent of life. Very fine are they that hold and endure above the ever flowing water that runs so fast.

Three days later, obsequies are in the past, whether one likes it or not.

The following days saw the barons arrive to pay homage and the renewal of their fiefs from the hands of their new lord, the young Count Bertrand, graceful and slim.

Raymondin would have preferred not to attend these meetings. His grief was not assuaged and he was hard put to overcome it, no doubt because, without being entirely responsible, he knew only too well what he had done and yet had to live alone with his secret. He felt a constant desire to leave. But nonetheless, he carried out unerringly the orders of she who had told him to stay.

When the last baron had paid homage to the count, another divine service celebrated their condition, this time at St Hilaire, where the great bell tower, later struck down in the course of a siege, still rose boldly with its steeple rising high over the building with seven naves. Here he took his turn, humbly, and in the formal language appropriate to all solemn circumstance declared:

"My lords, noble barons of the county of Poitiers, I request and pray that you give good ear to the request that I address to my lord the Count. And if it seems according to reason, that you join with me in wishing that he deign to grant it."

The barons agreed.

Then in the great hall of lordly arms with bare walls, decorated a little below the roof with the arms of the surrounding castles, he knelt before the throne where Count Bertrand sat, on a thick red carpet with regular geometric designs, yellow around a radiant golden sun, and said:

"Most dear and respected lord, I humbly request that in recognition of the service rendered by me to your noble father, whose soul is with God – and already close to Him – it would please you to grant me a gift that will cost you nothing. I wish to ask of you, in fact, neither for town, nor castle nor fortress…"

"If it pleases my barons," the young count interjected, "it will also please me."

"Sire," these others assured him, "since it is a thing of such small value, we can hardly refuse it, as he has so well and loyally served Count Aimery. We agree to it."

And taking off the right gauntlet, as many had already done, each raised his bare right hand.

"So let it be according to your word. Since we are all agreed, I grant your request. Speak boldly Raymondin."

"Great thanks, generous lord and may grace be rendered to you. I ask no other gift of you than to grant me, above the Fountain of Thirst and around it, in the forest of Colombier, as much space as could be encompassed by the hide of a stag."

"By the white robe of the Holy Father is that all you ask? I grant it willingly. I will even add that you need pay no homage for it, either to me or my successors, and thus no rent or dues whatever."

The gift definitely granted, Raymondin kneeled a second time, with the same humility before his lord. Then, having given thanks, he requested confirmatory letters and charters that guaranteed it to him formally.

Next day these were duly presented to him from Count Bertrand's own hands. They were on fine parchment, sealed with the Count's great seal as well as the different seals of the twelve peers. These, with their fine wax of diverse colours and imprinted designs, were a magnificent sight. They came in all forms, for the most part round or in lozenge shape, and their décor, like their lines, recalled the images of stained glass windows but more regular and heraldic. Raymondin found there the arms he knew best and had seen on the doublets in the cheerfulness of the morning they departed joyfully for the terrible hunt. But suppressing that painful memory – as he was accustomed to do from now on – he read the parchments from which fell ribbons, half red, half blue, attached to the seals.

One seal of black carried a lion of silver embroidered with a crown of gold; another a black Moor's head turbaned with silver, and supported by two blue thrushes and heads of beasts in red; another of silver with three rugged green tree trunks; yet another of blue with a horizontal band of gold accompanied by three sheaves of corn and a border of red charged with eight silver roundels; another of blue with a silver wild cat having in its jaws a black mouse, and red at the point of the shield, with four silver pieces up from the base; one of blue again, with a golden hawk catching a partridge with beak and members of red; finally one of red on the right and silver to the left, with a closed fist grasping two falcons, the one to the right of green, that to the left of purple, their heads facing, and bordered with blue.

Five other plaques had been badly struck or loosely held in the mould, or with the wax insufficiently hot; but there was no cause to fear error.

·V·

Possessing the Land

On his way out of the abbey of Moutiers, where he had come on the morning of his departure to pray until the hour of prime, Raymondin met a man carrying a deer skin round his shoulders. Seeing him, the man approached, intent on stopping him, and asked if he wanted to buy the deer skin, which would make good strong cords for huntsmen.

"How much is it?"

"A hundred sols sir."

"Come to my rooms, my friend, and I will pay you."

He returned to Poitiers with the man, and at his lodgings paid the agreed sum for the deer skin. The man departed happy, and Raymondin went off to a saddler to whom he explained:

"I want you, as soon as possible, to cut this skin as fine as you can, in fact finer than you have ever done before. Fine, very fine, into a long strip, hardly the thickness of a horse hair, that will stretch a long long way – but taking care you don't break it."

The saddler set to, quickly and skilfully. The skin, having been cut very fine – but strong, for it was a deer skin – Raymondin put into a sack that he hoisted on the shoulders of the saddler. Then he went to find the men commissioned by the young count to deliver his gift.

They left Poitiers on horseback and did not stop until they had reached the mount rising above Colombier. Here they were astonished to find that a wide trench had been dug, with a great felling of trees, around the great rock that overlooked the Fountain of Thirst. Although most surprised, and that agreeably, for Raymondin felt this must be the result of Melusine's orders, he affected to find everything quite normal. But as he looked over the meadow where he had recently plighted his future it seemed transformed, not only bigger, but somehow different, perhaps because it was now daylight.

They dismounted and began to empty the sack. The Count's surveyors were astonished even more when they saw the skin cut so finely. They vowed they had never seen one cut so cunningly, and did not know quite how to deal with it. As they were standing there, uncertain what to do, two strangers dressed in rough brown homespun appeared, and added to their astonishment when they said: "We have come to help you."

Straight away, before anyone could say a word, they unwound the skin from the heap where it lay coiled, and as if they knew exactly what to do, carried it to the bottom of the valley as close to the rock as possible. At a chosen place they planted a great stake to which they attached one end of the hide. Then taking, as and when required, smaller stakes from a bundle ready prepared, they planted them from place to place all around the rock. Example is often better than words when it comes to a job of work, and soon the others followed them, attaching the line to each baton. In this way they ended up having gone round the mount for a distance of two leagues.

The Count's men had no idea of the amount of space that could thus be enclosed by a simple deer skin. They measured it, shaking their heads and throwing up their hands. But they had seen nothing yet, for it is only necessary for one thing to start, and others follow. In the end they began to doubt their own reason, if not their very existence, as a brook sprang up in front of them. At least two paces wide, it flowed, clear and bubbling, making sweet sounds over little pebbles of fine gravel, across the valley. And where they also saw, within an hour, the towers of several mills. When they could take their eyes from it, which had opened so wide as almost to engulf their faces, they deliberated on what had occurred, but felt this was no time to discuss the matter. The text on the charter was precise. There was no way of avoiding it. They were obliged to assign to Raymondin the land enclosed by the circuit of the skin. That had been done. But when they turned to question the two strangers dressed in homespun, they found they had disappeared.

That brought discussion to an end, so they spoke only of going home. They rode back to Poitiers, as they had left it, followed by Raymondin.

They looked back frequently, observing him in silence, with a distrustful curiosity and some fear that he had somehow taken advantage of them. But he responded with a smile, keeping his distance from them, upright on his horse as a handsome knight should be. At the entrance to the town, they saluted him politely, left him without a word and pressed on to warn their master of the strange things they had seen at the Fountain of Thirst.

Bertrand received them while in counsel with his mother, who sighed reflectively:

"There must have been some spell or trickery. Those woods of Colombier hold either a den of thieves or a miracle; it is not the first hint of magic that has come from there. Whatever way you look at it, what happened was far from normal."

"You are right," replied her son. "What they have told us is stranger than anything that has happened before. I don't mind sorcery, apart from its possible menace. On the other hand, I don't understand it. But on one point, at least, I am sure: Raymondin is a loyal knight. And I pray God, for his sake as well as mine, that all turns out to his honour, with a fortunate outcome."

So they conversed, when he of whom they spoke arrived, according to the old adage that if you talk of the devil you will soon see his tail.

"By the Holy Blood," cried the Count, "am I glad to see you!"

"And I you sir," replied Raymondin, putting knee to the ground on the beautiful carpet where the greyhounds lay stretched, without moving their eyes, their muzzles at their master's feet like extensions of his pointed shoes. "To reaffirm my loyalty and to thank you, with all my heart, for the great gift you have bestowed on me."

Count Bertrand smiled slightly, then said, "It was nothing. If it pleases God, the supreme Lord of all, I would give you yet more. But on this point, young sir, as my late father liked to call you, I have heard surprising things about the land you asked for. You are of noble blood, so pray tell me the whole truth of the matter."

"Most dear and respected Lord," replied Raymondin, with gracious ease, "if your men have told you what they saw, they have done well, for they simply told the truth – that the deer skin, when cut, extended for more than two leagues. And they know as much as you or me about the two men dressed in homespun who came to help us. As for the rest, like the stream and the mills, do not ask me, for I know no more than you."

As a well born son Bertrand knew his role. He turned his eyes towards his mother, fixed them for some seconds on his vassal, then, because he loved him, resolved not to push his questioning further. He was reluctant to burden him with his suspicions, such as they were. Better to believe him for now and take him at his word. Also he wanted to give him the accolade as he left, the better to show his affection, and having given it to receive the same.

Eager to return to Melusine, Raymondin quickly gathered his baggage and left in the afternoon.

His horse went quickly, spurred by the passion it felt from its rider, as the woods of Colombier drew nearer. When he arrived at the Fountain of Thirst he saw a kind of building, tall and well constructed, which he had never seen before. On approaching, he saw several maidens, beautifully dressed, with carefully coiffed hair under their pointed headdresses, and accompanied by squires. They came toward him respectfully as if he were their lord, and gathered round him in welcome.

"Sir," they said, curtseying low, "pray dismount and come to meet our Lady, and also your own, who awaits you."

All seemed so normal that he kept his surprise to himself in the face of this detailed and lifelike reality and tried to accept everything quite naturally without showing alarm. He followed on foot those who led him, who looked back from time to time to renew their marks of respect, happy to know he was approaching Melusine.

He joined her in a splendid hall, bigger and finer even than that of the Castle at Poitiers, where she appeared to reign over the other lords and ladies. She had risen as soon as she saw him and came to take him by the hand. Everyone bowed as they passed between the two ranks of heralds at arms with colours half sky blue, half white, with an escutcheon of bat's wings over a star, under orange coloured banners, with white or gold suns and stars, marked in diverse ways with astrological signs. On a dais, of a darker blue than that of the heralds, and embroidered with silver, was a kind of bed of the same material. She invited him to sit by her and then with a simple gesture, dismissed all the company. When the last little page, who looked back to steal a glance at them, and then the last dwarf, who as was his way, shook the little bells on his cap and pulled a face as he closed the door, had both gone, she opened her arms to embrace him. He clasped her in turn, neither able to satisfy their desire in this mutual embrace. When they had finished almost suffocating each other she whispered that she had not yet had time to look at him properly. He acceded for fear of displeasing her, and she gazed deeply upon him.

"I know you have done all I asked you to do. And through my love and your own be assured that all will be well."

"I have found such a good fortune in following your words that I can no longer doubt the need to obey whatever you ask from now on."

But she perceived that his words contained, if hidden, a certain reservation, and reassured him.

"Good times, now and for ever. But have no fear! I would ask nothing of you that was not honourable and desirable for you and for me – above all for you – and all will come to a good end."

Then they returned to themselves and their love for each other, but as they began to talk of it a great blow resounded on the door of the hall. A knight entered and kneeled ceremoniously.

"My lady, all is ready," he announced from the doorway, "whenever you please."

They passed into an even bigger hall where two pages offered them golden jugs of perfumed water with which to rinse their hands. They sat face to face at a table overlooking the others, occupied by knights and ladies finely dressed and splendidly jewelled. An orchestra that seemed invisible could be heard, composed of mandores, rebecs, bass viols and lutes. It came from behind a carved wooden balcony near the ceiling at one end, that concealed the mysterious musicians. As for the waiters, they were so many and served so skilfully that they astonished and delighted the lord for whom all this was laid on.

"Where do they all come from, my love?" he asked.

"These knights and ladies are at your command," replied Melusine. "No one is here who does not seek to serve you, beginning with me. There are many more whom you have not yet seen, but whom you will come to know when you wish, for they belong to you."

At times he wondered if he was not in the middle of a dream as the most delicious dishes continued to be offered until he could eat no more.

Grace said, and dinner finished, hands washed under the red gold jugs, the diners retired and Melusine led Raymondin into her bedroom, as prepossessing as herself, where a good fire of dry logs and fir cones burnt under a great stone chimney place, with two fine seats under its mantle.

As he admired the contents of the room and breathed in the atmosphere impregnated with vervain, she took from a silver purse inlaid with gold at her waist a long key, the tines of which were designed in the form of two hearts united by a cross. She bent over a large chest at the foot of the bed, and while she engaged the key in the heavily engraved lock he admired the similar design on the polished wood, corresponding to that on the lock with discrete interlacing many times repeated.

She took from the chest a long cloak of violet silk with a border of black leaves, and at the waist a fine belt of pale gold with supple rings. As she proffered it to him she offered to divest him of some of his clothes. He was pleased to let her do so, regretting only that she did not go further, feeling all the more at ease in the soft decorated amaranthine silk. This was also due to something very subtle, impalpable, more discrete than vervain, and was, no doubt, the fragrance of Melusine herself, impregnating and sweetening all in that beautiful room, from its walls of neutral tints to the great curtains, violet like his robe, at each side of the two long windows, as the fire from the chimney blazed up in its own vibrant colour.

All this served to draw the two of them together and toward the great low bed covered with furs. But it was he, above all, who pressed Melusine, whose beauty, in his eyes, became more and more overpowering as she murmured:

"Dear friend, let us think about our marriage."

"I think of nothing else, as you can well see! I have not ceased to want you since the hour we met."

But she kept her head, and at such times it is certain that a woman knows best.

"You cannot marry me just like that Raymondin. Our love must not be celebrated as if we were ashamed of it. It must be affirmed before everyone, and to be sure of that, we must invite Count Bertrand, his mother, his sister, his friends and yours. They will bring honour to our marriage and it will give equal honour to them, as I will show. And as they must not suppose you are marrying beneath you, you may tell them you are taking to wife the daughter of a king."

And as he continued to be more occupied with what he wanted rather than by the counsels he was hearing, she insisted:

"So go now. As quickly as you did on your first journey, the sooner to return to me."

"So I will, Lady! But the better to plead our cause, Melusine, it is necessary I take the sacrament…

And kneeling at her feet, he caressed her hands and her arms and then her long shapely legs, fit to damn the wisest prince. His kisses worked their way up her silken stockings beyond their silver garters with golden buckles. What he said inbetween times was so ardent and tender, what he suggested so natural, that she dared not admit that her desire responded to his. She hardly knew any longer how to resist. For one last time she tried to repulse him, but he was already kissing her beautiful thighs. Then, not wanting to deny him any more, and happy to give herself, she helped him remove the rest of her clothes, crying:

"Take me then, you wretch! Since you desire me as much as I want you!"

Invitation to the Wedding

aymondin left next morning not only sure that he loved Melusine but knowing that she possessed all that was needed to be his wife.

But the nearer he got to Poitiers and fellow human beings, the more unbelievable his good fortune appeared to be – even though he knew it to be so real. And if recalling the rapture of possessing Melusine encouraged him, he realised the difficulty in talking about it and making others understand. Hesitation was impossible, even if it entered his mind, so he was happy to arrive before having to debate too long with himself about what could not be delayed. He asked for an immediate audience with the Count, whose welcome reassured him in deciding to explain himself straightaway.

"Most dear Sir, in view of the duties I owe to you, I pray that on the first day of next week you come to my wedding, with your mother, your sister and all your court. It will take place at the Fountain of Thirst you so generously gave me."

Count Bertrand could not conceal his astonishment.

"Good cousin, do you think yourself such a stranger as to choose a wife without consulting me? I would judge it disappointing if I did not think it incomprehensible! I was surprised at things that have already been reported to me, but am amazed at what you now have to say. How couldn't I be? To find myself the last to hear about this news? Did it not occur to you that I should be the first you turn to for advice in these matters?"

"Dear good lord, your anger shocks me, and would grieve me if I did not see it as proof of your affection. Love is my only excuse, for Love has such total power that He makes things happen even to those who would rather reflect before they acted. So pity me and congratulate me, and by your understanding or your mercy keep me as your own. I have gone so far I that cannot draw back. What is more, I would not, if all the powers in the world ordered me to. I seek, my Lord, to answer the call of flesh and blood, of body and soul, there where my whole life is, now and forever."

Count Bertrand pulled back a little.

"I do not recognise you any more," he murmured sadly.

He saw him, at the same time, as too far gone to listen to reason. He paused, then put the next question.

"At least tell me whom you love to this extent, and her lineage."

Shuddering for the fate of a dream which his lord and master seemed inclined to dismiss, but remaining calm, fixed, and courageously focused on his purpose, Raymondin answered:

"You ask me the one thing that I cannot answer. Because you need to know something else – I have not asked her!"

"By the black plague", cried Bertrand, now visibly angry, "this is the maddest thing I ever heard! You are getting married and do not know to whom!"

Danger increased Raymondin's confidence. And knowing that the hardest had been said encouraged him the more. His words were filled with persuasive conviction in their audacity.

"By the living God, Sir, since what I have done and know about pleases me, should that not be enough? Women do not enter the destiny of men often, unless they can do something that not even Providence is able to change. It accepts them for what they are, along with those whom they cherish and who love them in return. What is love, tell me, noble sir, if not an enchantment? It works through charms that are infallible even when they deceive, sometimes indeed *because* of that! I do not take a wife for you, or for another, but for myself. What am I to do then? Who can take exception? In whose name, or by what power? I will bear the grief or the blessings that please God. Since He has not forbidden me this far, have I not the right to believe that He protects us, not only me but her? And so would it not offend Him not to go on? In the end, surely this only concerns me!"

"You speak well and subtly, Raymondin," replied the Count, with something of a sneer at first but then beginning to laugh, "and I will follow you, or at least, try my best! I must say I admire you, and she who advises you, even though I do not know her. She has made you into a good advocate who renders twist for turn to entrap the most experienced... Although if the God you invoke be Love himself, who, the ancients said, was born blind or blindfold, I would fear for my personal future even whilst I said my prayers. Obviously I do not care for your folly, if folly it is, but I would not refuse the advantage if advantage there is in it. You have said what you have been told. I accept that. And I pray your patron saint will protect you, and that God will bless you throughout your adventure. My anxiety comes from my head rather than my heart, which continues to move me and is entirely concerned for your welfare. But to show that I hold no ill will in this matter, I will come to your wedding, with all my family and court, as you have asked. I am curious, as you may guess, to meet and even to love your wife. Gentle, audacious and foolish cousin, if I find you happy, with all the elements of good fortune, be sure that I will be the first to say so!"

"That delights and rewards me, Sir," cried Raymondin, putting knee to ground and kissing the great jewelled ring on the Count's hand, the one that had belonged to his father and which he had put on only that day, and which appeared to his vassal to be a good augury. "Accept my greatest thanks. I am most happy for you to meet my Lady for I am sure she will please you well."

"I hope so too."

Count Bertrand rose, took him by the arm, and they left, talking of other things, until suppertime.

Next day, after mass, the Count called all his people and told them of Raymondin's marriage, its imminence, and his resolve to take them there. He included Raymondin's brother, the Count of Forez, whom the latter had forgotten to mention, either because he would have done so later or for some other unspoken reason.

After this news all looked on Raymondin with a curiosity that grew greater the more they questioned him. He was so bound up with thoughts of Melusine, her beautiful body and what they had done together, that this evocation of happiness shone in his face. All who questioned him laughed at the display of such felicity, so rare, so radiant in its fullness. None could conceive such love to be so complete, but even the most persistent smiles faded as both men and women began to doubt, or at least to question themselves about their own first judgement, and their own loves.

When the time came to leave, each reflected deeply about what they might be going to see. As for Raymondin, he recalled, when looking at them, the departure for the terrible hunt. Hardly ten or twelve days before but so full of incident that it seemed three or four times as long – along with what had since happened in such extraordinary ways. Things that he could not have conceived in his wildest imagination. And as evening fell, he saw once more, even more clearly, old Aimery under the stars, head back, with his white beard lengthening his face, parallel to earth and sky. He asked himself if the Count had not then seen all that was going to happen, even the loss of his life, and if, in his good will he had done nothing about it, so as not to change the fine destiny of the nephew he loved. Now, having seemed so close to him, he felt the old Count himself right behind him on the back of his horse, and as he turned his head, felt it seized as if between two icy stones, and a kiss, as cold as those stones, pressed upon his forehead. He shivered, but, at the same time, was overcome with great comfort. Hot tears of gratitude flowed down his cheeks as he murmured: "My sweet lord, to whom I owe all by your death, and who now absolves me, why can you not return to be here? I would hold you in my arms with such delight!" But as he did so the old Count raised a hand, put a finger to his lips, and then disappeared, leaving Raymondin convinced that Melusine had been right to insist upon silence. And fortified with an amazing burst of self confidence he felt himself to be the master of his fate.

On the night journey all were prey to their own fancies lurking in the shadows. The forest seemed to reveal a totally unknown form of life. No doubt that of its familiars, profiting from the darkness, for daylight delivers too much power to men. These now become their masters once again. But those eyes that shone like still flames or disappeared suddenly behind leafless branches evoked the thought of invisible beings of a different nature, even the Devil himself. So more than one made the sign of the cross as a precaution, for how to know if these lights were of good or of evil? Beyond the light of the torches lit for supper within a ring of lances stuck into the ground, it would certainly have been a question of the usual beasts. For one could have seen them returning little by little, the flashing eyes a little way off, unmoving. And as the fire grew bigger, gradually revealing in the light of the flames, the paws, the still bodies, waiting for the end of the meal and the departure of those who partook of it. But at the last brimful glass of mead, a page dressed in green like the coming Spring, a little squire of the Lord of Forez, had not been able to restrain himself from taking up his bow. He was a good marksman, for his arrow struck a great wolf right between the eyes, whose fall and raucous cry made all the other Ysengrims flee. Perhaps it was because of fear of possible vengeance that on resuming their passage, men and women stuck closer together, reluctant to wander apart or fall behind the cavalcade. In fact the burning eyes were so many, silent in the darkness of the night, that other presences seemed on the point of showing themselves. Even nobler beasts – for a little before dawn the leech, Hesnin la Panouze, dozing under his fox skin cap with ear flaps, and unconscious of the danger, fell behind the last of the rearguard on his mule. But on rejoining the escort, he assured all that he had been awakened suddenly by the swift passing of Brechemir, the great stag with high antlers, followed by eight hinds – (was he bragging or truly precise?) – and their fawns – (of which he had not been able to recall the number) – in full flight.

In order to please everyone and increase his importance, at least in his own eyes, the leech added that, without wishing to specify all that he had seen exactly, he regarded this memorable encounter, rare at such an hour, the happiest of omens, the first blessing on the wedding and of the happy couple themselves. He saw himself supplanting Arbatel, the astrologer whose influence had waned since the sad end of the old Count, for which he had been thought responsible, being too much inclined to magic sciences. All the same Hesnin relished his easy success a little too much, with his knowing and patronising airs, especially towards the ladies, who only laughed at him.

·VII·

The Marriage Feast

The sun had risen to shine on a cold morning in a clear sky, still tinted with dawn, when Raymondin, who had not been able to restrain himself from taking the lead, saw the vast trenches that had recently been made, as exclamations rose from those behind him at these extensive works. The stream, above all, made some nearly fall off their horses. Huntsmen and fishermen who knew the place could not recall its previous existence. One old fisherman of Count Aimery rubbed his eyes, not sure whether he was asleep and dreaming all this. He got down from his horse and leaned over the clear running water, his old ardour revived, to calculate his chances of a catch if he returned next day.

Little flat freshwater fish with silver sides swam in single file among the lively minnows; a fat chub, a large roach, and a perch, all passed up and down as they were wont to be there. All this little aquatic world seemed happy, until a great barbell, that appeared to sleep in the depths among the golden bream, rose to a band of minnows like a flash of lightning, jaws open, and swallowed some while the others scattered.

"By St Christopher," the fisherman exclaimed, "if my lord's cousin isn't bewitched – and may St Michael forgive me – I think we must be as well!"

Many tents were spaced about the meadow, and as the procession approached, the whole court came out to salute Raymondin. Count Bertrand was astonished at all this, then raising his eyes, stared open mouthed, a cry of surprise strangled in his throat. On the summit of the rock of the Fountain of Thirst, as if grown from the very rock, a chapel stood with a steeple rising like an arrow toward the sky.

Marvels came so thick and fast that they began to seem quite natural – the people, the earthworks, the building, imposing their own reality upon initial astonishment.

Bertrand and Raymondin rode side by side, the lord glancing surreptitiously at his vassal as, not far from the Fountain of Thirst, a knight came to meet them. Mounted on a great horse he had a sage and antique air, with strangely unfashionable clothes, yet splendid in form and embellished with gold fastenings. Two men at arms escorted him a short distance away, their armour dark and sombre but extremely beautiful.

Their horses were decked in dark red robes, and that of the old knight with a sort of silvery silk.

He addressed Raymondin first, saluting low.

"My lord, I request you take me to the Count of Poitiers, for I needs must speak with him."

And when Raymondin replied "He is here before you, at my side," the knight addressed him with the following ceremonious words:

"Sire, the most powerful and noble lady Melusine of Albany commends herself to your Highness, and thanks you for the great honour you have granted your cousin in coming to witness their marriage."

The count remained silent for a moment, then replied quickly, not without sign of a little irritation.

"There is no need to thank me for that. I do what I must in friendship to my cousin. I thought I knew my county, yet never knew until today I lived so near a noble lady with such a numerous company."

The old knight replied simply: "Ah, Sire, if it pleases my Lady, when she wants she can have many more. She has but to wish in order to have them."

Count Bertrand thought she was very lucky and was about to say so, but the old knight now helped him to dismount and conducted him to the entrance of a tent. All within was sumptuous, to the point that the count and his court could hardly believe their eyes. All were installed in superb rooms where they found servers and servants to their need, attentive and smiling. There were even various jesters, in clothes of many colours, who came to offer their services in case any of the guests felt sad. But, as they discovered none, the gaily coloured band retired in order and in silence shaking their cap and bells.

There was no one who was not filled with admiration. Especially the widow of the Count of Poitiers and her daughter, housed in a pavilion furnished in cloth of gold ornamented with pearls and precious stones. Their wonder grew greater when the old knight presented them to Melusine and she offered them a casket full of jewels. Talking later to her son, who still had his doubts, Count Aimery's widow avowed that she had never ever seen a lady so fresh, so genteel or beautiful.

On her wedding day, Melusine appeared more beautiful than ever. Her dress seemed more splendid than that of any queen or empress. Her face more radiant than the silver embroidery on the blue velvet and white gauze, more fresh and clear than the lilies that decorated the altar, more delicate than the rose petals that the children threw before her as she walked. Above all was her happy grace and charm, for there is nothing more becoming than happiness. On her long wide sleeved tunic lined with ermine, the Alençon lacework, which covered all, enveloped her like an aureole. Her long fair hair, gathered over her ears under her headdress, shone brighter than her golden belt and the alms purse that hung from it. The whole sky, all the springs and the whole sea seemed present in her blue eyes, wide and sweet and deep, beneath eyelids lightly tinted with the tone of elm and poplar leaves when autumn begins to fix upon them the caresses of the sun. Her smile was a living perfection of the red of cherries and crimson of the wild rose. The pure oval of her face, so regular and smooth, the soft ivory of an almond, that recalled the saints at the portal of Notre Dame la Grande, or the antique statues of nymphs which the Saracens had brought to the court of Poitiers in the time of Aimery, on the advice of Arbatel. The leech Hesnin la Panouze declared pedantically to his familiar pupils that she represented Nature, and united in herself all the charms and gifts of Nature that her happy spouse would possess that evening between the sheets, there to sanctify it, at the feet of God, by making another, very different, use of it!

The Count of Poitiers and the Count of Forez led her to the altar. Raymondin followed, a fine figure, on the arm of the Countess. A long procession thus mounted toward the chapel of Notre Dame de Soif – which was the name by which it was henceforth called. The heralds at arms who preceded them, not pausing for breath, responding to each other with their long trumpets from which hung large embroidered pennants with fringes of gold and silver thread.

The chapel, hung with draperies and illuminated with candles, seemed a great open reliquary to the ecstasy of the living of this world. A bishop with the sacerdotal ornaments of violet robe, short and simple mitre, cross in hand, appeared like a pale and canonised saint expressly descended from paradise to bless the couple. The great central rose window rayed the sunlight with all the symbolic colours of its panes upon the crowd. The harmonies of the organ recalled the voice of the forest and of the wind upon the plain or over the waves. And the voices raised, even though human, combined so perfectly with the breath of the long organ pipes that they seemed a foretaste of angelic harmonies that come from unknown spheres.

When the mysterious bishop took two gold rings from a red cushion and placed one on the finger of Melusine and the other on that of Raymondin, even the most doubtful were convinced that this astonishing and magnificent marriage was the most beautiful and most religious that had ever been seen, and celebrated in a true place of worship according to divine law.

The feast that followed increased their trust and raised their enthusiasm. It was served in the great hall where Raymondin had already feasted, but which now appeared to him at least three times even larger yet.

On long tables, decked with primroses, anemones and daffodils, pitchers of all kinds, bottles of crystal and silver jugs were aligned with great metal vases, and great handled plates with spatulas, spoons and knives. Before each guest were numerous goblets of different kinds for the different wines, some of ivory or horn encircled or encrusted with metal, others of rock crystal, decorated silver and red. Music featuring flutes, violas de gamba and violas d'amore, was provided by groups of minstrels in the four corners of the room and the gallery. And when everyone was placed, with Raymondin and Melusine face to face, the music stopped.

A majestic majordomo, accompanied by three ushers, and followed by an immense troop of servants, came into the middle of the hall through the swing doors from the kitchens. He saluted, and advanced, a fine ebony wand headed with a silver pine cone in his hand, and asked respectfully for silence. Then he pulled a long parchment decorated with seals from beneath his blue and green tunic which he wore especially for the purpose of making an announcement, and with great solemnity and pauses for applause, read out the list of dishes.

When he had finished, he went back to announce the first dish again, that all had forgotten by now. This was trout fried in oil on a purée of crushed almonds, and servants soon entered carrying them, while on the threshold, each dish was examined by the six chefs who had prepared them, each with the aid of a thick short horn wand bearing cabalistic signs to banish malefic influence. They had also prepared at one side a round table at which no one sat, provided with exquisite wines and cakes, and seven empty cups and seven white loaves for the fairies.

After patés of pimparneaux, there was red roast partridge under the fat on laurel leaves, seasoned with cloves and ginger and stuffed grouse. Fattened chickens and geese followed, the latter on cooked liver, surrounded by egg yolks, the first on rounds of onion and in a spiced stock. Long and blue pike, cold, but mixed in a sauce of cooked white wine, dotted with grains of pepper, alternated with dishes of eels as a digestive aid to the fowls. During this interlude pots of mead, already frequently replaced, ceded for a time to a white wine of the Loire, light, very dry, which soothed the stomach and cleared the head.

Then the most handsome men among the servers brought in an enormous boar, cooked slowly on a spit, from which they had taken care to collect the sauce; it was poured on each piece of the beast, served on grilled bread, seasoned with vinegar and cloves, and the juice flavoured with juniper.

(Some chagrined spirits found this course in bad taste, in remembrance of Count Aimery, and there was a diminution of liveliness, but only for a moment.) With these delicious meats, goblets of rock crystal received an old wine of Poitou, flavoured and seasoned like a bouquet of carnations.

Then, after a short pause, the valets reappeared, carrying on their heads roast peacocks with the feathers of their tails spread out in a fan. On the raised arms of those who carried them, they seemed to fly across the hall.

At the table where the happy couple sat a bigger one was carried. When it had been placed before Raymondin, Melusine took it by the neck and as she raised it, there arose from the plate a live white peacock that flew round the hall before alighting on the edge of the gallery. Then, at a signal, the music, which had ceased after the venison, recommenced, and one of the chefs opened the large middle window, through which the peacock took flight, over the close cut green lawn to a far terrace where it settled on a sundial of marble and bronze.

All marvelled when the jugglers entered, throwing great bowls of opaque crystal up to the ceiling, against which they broke to release pigeons among perfumed sweetmeats and scented dried rose leaves, while from the great decorated chimney under the gallery turtle doves flew: the two flights meeting and winging their way up to the peacock on the green lawn where, in the distance, they seemed to swoop like great living daisies.

Crayfish, that swam in their court-bouillon, were passed in enormous bowls of plain dark red earthenware emphasising their lively colour. They were seasoned with glassfuls of Rhine wine, in which the taste of fire stone helped to reawaken the appetite. Then after rails, plovers and even curlews fricasséed with turnips, there were little golden pigs baked in a prune sauce. While to finish, birds' livers accompanied with saffron cooked rice.

The first deserts then appeared, the wine waiters pouring out Cyprus wine, wine of aloes in which was hidden a few drops of the elixir of long life, and an avalanche of fruits, conserved no-one knew how, as fresh as if they had been picked but yesterday. Tarts, cakes, cinnamon biscuits and creams, among which were snow eggs perfumed with a herb and angelica liquor that had been brought expressly from an old Italian convent, whose monks possessed the secret from time immemorial; who from one of the highest peaks of the Abruzes descended at night to gather the simples that composed it at dawn on certain lunar dates in impenetrable valleys known only to themselves. As for the angelica, it was prepared and guarded in a little laboratory room entered only by the father priors, who passed on the recipe before they died.

Now all the servers, the valets, the kitchen staff and chefs disappeared. There remained only the big majordomo who had changed his fine ebony wand with the silver pine cone for one of horn, but longer and tipped with a golden arrow head. He hurled it against the far end wall at a required point which made two doors swing open, through which entered pages whose fine legs were clad in tights of violet silk with dark red skin-tight tunics up to the neck. They carried pasties in the form of castles.

When they had served them to all the tables, they ranged behind the guests in ranks, face to face, and raised their caps. Then that which many had guessed took place. Their long hair uncovered, one dark, one fair, the length of the hall, it descended to their shoes – the young men were maidens after all!

The leech Hesnin la Panouze was so much enthused by the one who stood behind him that he could not resist avowing loudly, as he put his knife in the golden crust of a pasty, that there was something else he would willingly break open, despite his age! But while he turned hastily to judge the effect of his words, he must have noticed their lack of influence. The maiden assigned to his service did not budge any more than a water god, her immobile face, with blue eyes, wide open under her black hair, remained fixed on the agate ones of the blonde one who faced her.

Then there were pasties of honied glacé fruits of all kinds, with dragées, bonbons and pastilles, sweets of glazed apples, cherry plums and quinces, and finally, oranges appeared.

The most vast cake had been placed on the central table before Raymondin, so great in size that it was even higher than his head when he stood before it. As he attacked the citadel, the walls were struck with a blow and a much alarmed hare came out from one side, and three black dwarves from the other. Then at the other end six more white dwarves arose, with baskets of flowers that they offered to the guests, marching on the tables and across the plates, jugs and goblets.

At the same time, supported by the minstrels softly playing, the maidens sang a song of welcome, calling for the happiness of the guests and thanking them for being here. It asked them to prolong their stay and to consider that their living quarters and all they found therein belonged to them, as well as all within the hall.

More than one turned to contemplate the maidens who gave such agreeable counsel and the grey beard leech Hesnin la Panouze wiped his mouth, which began to dribble, with the hair of the one behind him. But her opulent mane, so black that it appeared blue, made his beard appear yet more white.

The majordomo with a just and advised nod, estimated it was time to bring things to an end. He bowed towards Melusine and Raymondin, who rose to lead out their guests to an interlude for games. The moment the guests pushed back their chairs, the young maidens offered each one a chaplet of flowers formed into a crown with carnations, marguerites, mint, renunculus, soucis, honeysuckle and artemesia.

·VIII·
Games of the Men

The day was already advanced, and popular games were set out in great tents of purple cloth under the sheltering elm tree. Much welcome, as in view of the recent mourning it had been decided there would be no jousts or tourneys. But the trouvères were many. Among them were some who promenaded slowly, riding oxen draped in scarlet while rendering their songs. Another had an ass covered in a violet robe, the same shade as that of the bishop, but embroidered with silver like that of an emir. On its back, in a little golden casket like a temple, was a manuscript of Pierre de Corbie in honour of the ass of Bethlehem. The trouvère sang these lines from it as the Count of Forez was passing:

> *Hic in collibus Sichem*
> *Jam mutritus sub Ruben,*
> *Transiit par Jordanem*
> *Salut in Bethleem*
> *Aurum de Arabia*
> *Thus et myrrhum de Saba,*
> *Tulit in ecclesia,*
> *Virtus Asinaria!*

Groups formed by chance, or according to mutual interests, discovered during the banquet, of preferences for different games. Most took dice from their pockets, little cubes of ivory or bone, picked out with dark points, even though there were some already provided on side tables along with shakers. Passion for dice was great, and more than one in this way lost not only his fortune, his means, his honour, but even his boots or his coat. Thus for many the dice were the snares of Evil. But how to condemn them? Dice had been allowed to St. Peter for the ransom of souls, and during the game, a trouvère walked round the ladies reciting the fable of the celestial Gatekeeper and the Juggler, where he who had given his name to the great church in Rome was represented with a dice shaker in his hand.

In the land of Sens death had surprised a poor minstrel in a state of mortal sin. Led straight to hell, the harper excited the pity of the Devil, for he was debauched beyond all imagination, and rendered Lucifer sympathetic as he had become so entirely without malice and purely for pleasure. Thus the Great Invisible Lord whom he now contemplated face to face (not without fear) entrusted him with the job of stoking the ovens where the damned were boiled for ever without dying. The minstrel, still chilled to the bone from his last nights under the stars, far from the beloved sinners who were his only source of warmth, greatly rejoiced.

"Have no fear," he said to his new prince, "I will guard your victims whenever you send them."

As the funerary king flew off with his acolytes to return to earth to execute what he called a general commotion, St. Peter came from his watch, introduced himself and winked, with three dice and a shaker in one hand, and gold and silver coins in the other – for the kingdoms of Death resemble those of Life.

St. Peter said to him, "Come along friend, bet five or six of those souls."

But the minstrel replied "Sir, I daren't. For if I lose one my master will surely eat me!"

The saint, without further comment, continued to make the heavenly coins ring and shook the dice. At length the minstrel could stand it no longer. Seizing the shaker, his eye on the money, then on the dice, he played. He played and lost without ceasing. The heavenly Gatekeeper quietly won souls, by dozens, by hundreds, soon by thousands, with great dexterity. He had no scruples about cheating, easing his conscience through serving a good, true and Christian cause. But the minstrel, less adroit and more nervous, no doubt because he now operated in hell, was also unfortunate because, in the face of such bad luck, without realising it, he sometimes overplayed his hand.

And the trouvère chanted the calling of all who, won by St. Peter, returned to the true and everlasting country: knights, ladies and canons, thieves, champions and monks, free men and villeins, many priests and chaplains – all passed there. So many indeed that on his return Satan found the cauldrons empty.

He threshed the watcher as dishonest and incorrigible and, convinced that he was good for nothing, with a terrible kick that would have broken his back and reduced his buttocks to dough if he had not been a soul, sent him back to God and the saints, in the midst of frightful imprecations from the demons, who swore on their forks and their shovels that no poet would ever enter hell again. Thus the depths of perdition had ended in creating health.

Then another trouvère, accompanied on a vielle in the style of Beri, sang the lines of Ruteboeuf:

THE WINTER DICE GAME
The dice that the dicers have thrown
Have stripped me down to the bone.
The dice have inflamed me,
Robbed me and blamed me,
Tempted and shamed me.

At little round tables players applauded or insulted each other in different ways, and with more or less fury, at the throw of the dice. Stamping and blaspheming went together, for the feasting and wine had inflamed their behaviour. They cared nothing for reputation or responsibility as they lost what they might win back a minute later, and in the heat of the moment the unhappy Virgin, the Saints and the Holy Father were as roughly handled as Beelzebub.

This led yet further. In another tent they had made a tight circle around two very fervent players, one of whom had thrown a heavy triangular iron chandelier with five tallow candles at the head of his opponent, who as he had not been stunned by the blow, grabbed the other by the throat. It was however, the only serious fight.

More happily philosophic, to judge from the noise, others were content with insults, injurious, even excremental, amid accusations of trickery or theft. It was, in fact, only game rage. Most altercations were resolved with a new pitcher of mead, or cassis steeped with cinnamon and nutmeg, or muscatel with cloves.

Loud of mouth and very much so in tongue, one of them, his cheeks scarlet and shiny as a pot, insisted on telling the story of how the first dice player had made up the rules. With bawling offensive voice he attributed the old "game of dice" to an unknown preacher, who in his wisdom ordained: "You make the dice of six square sides! On one of the faces you put one, in despite of God. On another two, in despite of Christ and Mary. On another three, in despite of the Holy Trinity. On another four, in disdain of the four evangelists. On another five, in spite of the five wounds of Jesus on the cross. And finally six on the last side, in despite of the six days that God made the world."

As they burst out laughing, most finding this funny, and promising themselves to remember it, he then, proud of his success, decided to show them the right way to drink. To do this, he opened his mouth very wide, threw back his head, and up-ended from on high, in a narrow jet, a pot of honey wine right down to the last drop.

Others exchanged thin golden ducats at what everyone knows as shove-halfpenny, the origin of which goes back to the first shepherds, who engraved compartments on a stone table, in the form of a square with median lines and diagonals, on which they played with three pebbles or jetons that had to be put in line. Others amused themselves at a game with pawns and dice on table divided into four compartments, which is our tric-trac or backgammon.

The wiser ones played chess, that they called "echiers", the invention of a famous ancient called Palamede that became a universal game. Once, in the Crusades, as told by Garin de Montglave, King Charles proposed a terrible game in which the stakes were, for him, his kingdom and his wife, and for Garin, nothing less than his own head. For the king knew that the queen loved Garin but without either of the two being culpable, so he could do nothing about this fine knight, in body, heart and soul, who sang:

> *Alas, what can I do if love overcomes me?*
> *How can I be blamed when God*
> *Who made my heart and mind*
> *Made love so sweet and pleasant?*

We also know, as told in *Huon of Bordeaux*, of his game of chess at the court of the Emir, where the beautiful invincible maiden let herself be beaten by the handsome knight, and then had no other wish than to fall into his arms to be vanquished a second time, in another fashion. Unfortunately he had such Christian faith that he failed to satisfy Esclarmonde.

This, to many, seemed extraordinary. Some, both men and women, reckoned this was just put on for outside show. That in fact they got on very well, and agreed to get together more than once and to say nothing. Otherwise, said the ladies, she would have forbidden him ever to return. But return he did.

Sitting apart from the others, Raymondin and his brother were finishing a serious game. The Count of Forez had invited him, almost dragged him there under the elm, and was visibly irritated as if about to lose. The chequered board was almost empty, and after a long pause Raymondin made a move with his Knight which the Count had not suspected. It checked his King, which could not move out of the line of a Rook or the reach of the Queen. He acknowledged in a discontented tone, that it was checkmate – which Raymondin had not cared to announce.

The count's whole bearing showed his disappointment, but nonetheless, forcing himself to smile, he took between two fingers the beautiful ivory figure of the Queen who had helped to mate him, and leaning towards his victor, threw at him abruptly a remark he had plainly had in mind for some time:

"Brother, you know my concern. All the more since I am your elder brother. Thinking about your actions today, it seems I must speak frankly. I am worried."

"What about and why?" asked Raymondin laughing.

"Should I tell you or keep it to myself?"

"Whatever it is, you must out with it."

"You think so?"

"Certainly. You have not brought me here just to say nothing."

"I will tell you then."

"As soon as you like, otherwise how can I know what bothers you?"

The count of Forez rose, the Queen in his hand, then sat down again, putting the piece on a black square, and leaned toward his brother, fixing him in the eye.

"She whom you have presented to us as your intended wife, who is not quite yet yours, but whom before God you aim to take as your own, is very beautiful."

"I know that, by my faith, and I don't complain about it! You neither, I think, if you love me?"

"Does she not astonish you?"

"Of course not, since she pleases me."

"Have you no fear for your happiness?"

"No, she satisfies me in every way."

"You do not fear a surprise, after all that has happened? Things which no one can understand?"

"Not a bit, except to be happier still!"

The Count of Forez lowered his eyes during these replies, but finished by observing his brother cautiously, who had not lowered his gaze. He now stared back at him, and taking up the Queen from the chess board again and toying with it, fixed his brother with an ironic smile.

"Then all is for the best?"

It was necessary to say something more, but Raymondin, now on his guard, remained silent.

The Count affected to contemplate the Queen. Finally putting it down, this time on one of the white squares of the little field of battle where she had recently triumphed, he said:

"Do you know, my brother, that, long ago, this piece was a man? And in the East, was subservient to the person of the King, and called the Minister? Then some, like certain people we know today, always gallant, even at games, but finding sex lacking in the two armies, pleaded against the King being alone, which is bad for a man. So in a certificate justly called the Writing, they changed the Minister to a Queen.

"Then, to spice up the game they freed up her moves – do not women always? And as they sought to increase her power, even when it had attained the limits, they married her to the King. Or opposed her to him, if you like. In any case charged her to defend him, as the good King could not successfully do so himself or alone. In short, they made the Queen the real ruler. And that is true, because with her aid you have just beaten me.

"Do you like my story? I'm sure it must please you."

Wrapped in the memory of a wondrous night of great delights, and sure that he was about to find them again, Raymondin smiled distantly, and said sweetly:

"Your story diverts me even more than my queen has me. Melusine is the daughter of a king, and I have won the game. I knew that already, brother. Now you have made me sure of it."

The Count of Forez could not suppress the deep resentment in his heart, and cried out, despite himself: "Only in today's game!"

·IX·
Diversions of the Ladies

The ladies soon tired of seeing the men swearing with such fury and were attracted by a crowd that stood at the door of one of the largest tents. They had lined up in rows but courteously made way for them. Two trouvères, turn and turn about, were currently singing of Garin de Montglave.

They told of his famous game of chess, a most moving drama and one of the best ever told. Of a kind like the players they had just left, but concerned with other things, less coarse, although quite frenzied, in the far East – embellished, what is more, with a love story, which made it all the more delectable.

The two young men, one rather thin and weedy, were still far short of thirty, which pleased those ladies who had not admitted to that age for some years. They described the preparation of the chess board, a masterpiece of ivory and precious stones, of which a single piece would be enough to enrich its possessor. The Cross of the Evangelist had been brought, upon which the two adversaries swore absolute honour, and their seconds placed themselves at their sides, amongst whom, for Garin, was the Duke of Aquitaine.

The Queen was lamenting plaintively, heart broken and accusing herself of being the cause of all this: "Alas! That they should be in conflict over my poor body!" Then the duel began.

In those days, the Rook was a Rock, and the Knight a Horseman. Within the first few moves of this immortal and memorable game, the King, with a Rock supported by a Horseman, thought he was about to mate. But Garin saw the trap, avoided it, and gained an advantage by taking the Horseman. The King was furious. The confined little mathematical space upon which he looked down, where nothing happened by chance, but where nonetheless all was uncertain and incomprehensible, already irritated him; now he was exasperated. Striking down with his fist, he scattered the pieces, pushed the board away from him, and threatened to make his opponent pay his debt before compline sounded.

Expecting something like this, Garin's supporters had good steel blades concealed under their hauberks which they now pulled out before the King. The Duke of what is now known as Normandy advanced toward Karle and solemnly reproached him for such a show of anger that all gentlemen present might think was madness. "I have a hundred men at arms here," he said, "who will not fail Garin in case of need."

Karle returned to the game without reply, but much more attentively. Silence returned. And continued. It weighed heavily on all and was frightening. The King started to play well again and now thought himself sure of the mate. Too much so, for he said so with brutal menace. Garin simply responded to these insults with a more subtle game, while the Count of Poitiers – a direct ancestor of Aimery and his son – taunted:

He thinks to distract our cousin with threats
But those are mere words, let the game take its course
He may find he has cause for much greater regrets
When he loses his King like he did his Horse.

Enraged, Karle seized a baton and threw it at the joker's head, so violently, that the apple wood would have killed him stone dead if he had not ducked. At this dishonourable act beyond the game, swords were drawn and Karle defended himself with an enormous club, of fir this time, but retreated along with four hundred of his vassals in arms when as many Chartrains and Angevins appeared. Blood cooled when, with eloquence and reason in equal measure, and good will, the Duke of Burgundy intervened.

The game started again, in silence from now on, but increasingly nerve wracking. Garin calculated his moves even more intensely. Luck was on his side. He conducted his game so well that mating the King was inevitable. Karle rose, hung his head, and admitted himself beaten.

But now Garin, moved by the humility of his Lord, declared he wanted to take nothing from him, neither his wife nor his land. But as he had not ceased to love, would die for it, by taking on an heroic folly that would hasten his end. There was a castle invincible and inaccessible high on the narrow summit of a range of sharp rocks with many mortal peaks and ravines. The final rock at such a height that it was rarely seen for clouds, whilst at other times, towering above those below it, it seemed to be floating upon them, unreal. Neither the bravest and best trained falcon nor even the mightiest eagle could hope to fly there.

No one had been able to dispossess those who held it despite the best prepared expeditions, and the greatest heroes had never returned. Not a single survivor nor even their bodies had been found. A mysterious master, all powerful, reigned there, taciturn, inexorable, sovereign prince of all the works of magic in the world, of whom this haunt was the aerial citadel. None had seen him, even his subjects, apart from their chiefs – who never spoke of him except between themselves.

For recompense, Garin asked permission to go and conquer it, on condition that he hold it in fief from Karle only, when and if he had taken it. The king opened his arms, wept and embraced him. He gave him his best horse, Abrive, that had no equal this side of the port of Carthage. Mounted on this fine beast, with its proud clear eyes almost of human intelligence, Garin left. The horse, as if winged, carried him to the summit of the rocks and invulnerable fortifications from where so many of the brave had fallen to their death.

At this point the ladies cried out and began such a lively discussion that the trouvères were soon forgotten and could not continue, ignored even by the older ones. Many ladies were shocked by what they heard. Garin de Montglave might be noble, but they felt him guilty of insufficient love. How could he reject it when it should be at its most powerful?

Some on the other hand, mostly young maidens far from any similar adventure, thought the story sublime. But most denied this, for they knew from experience that there are things, and especially love, which cannot be resisted by either side.

This was the trenchant advice of the leech Hesnin la Panouze who joined in the conversation, seasoning it with bawdy remarks that, for lack of some better way, he thought proved the permanent state of his youth, even though when he laughed smugly to the people he was talking to, his few remaining teeth were seen to be fretted with gold in order to stay in his head.

Many despised the knight. They declared him insulting toward the queen, who loved him so much, so humbly and beautifully, and that his unforeseen decision, so suddenly and brusquely announced, was inexcusable. They laughed at the tenderness of Karle for contenting himself with so little, for he must have realised he was no longer loved. And one of them was sure that after this it was impossible for the queen not to take a dislike to both men, and little by little to despise them.

The story, now legend, but nonetheless authentic, had been lived in the past, but the ladies came to view it in the present. As many knew, more or less from their own adventures, there were allusions that came a little too close to the truth. Consequently, wandering from the point, the better to avoid disturbing thoughts, silences began to grow between them that weighed a little heavily. Thus their attention returned to the two trouvères, so young and sheepish in the middle of all this prattle on matters beyond their understanding.

This reunited them and renewed their friendship. What is more they knew one of the youngsters was much in love with of one of them, who on discovering it had repulsed him severely, for reasons given by the poet:

Boy's love is not enough.
No lady can be cheered
If taken into the scrawny arms
Of one with a wispy beard

In the end, the lady observed the embarrassment of the sighing youth and also that all were looking at her. To avoid this attention and lead the others back to their own affairs, she decided on a game of Questions and, taking the first, asked the younger minstrel if had ever fathered a child.

Attacked so directly, he realised that nothing stopped him from replying in much the same way.

"Lady," he said, "if I had I would not boast about it!"

Piqued, she became cruel:

If you did I would not believe you
And in this I am not alone
For what can be gotten by a lad
Whose beard is barely grown?

Got at so heavily, he said nothing at first, but then asked in a fine and strong voice for a game of Attack and Defend. This changed the spirit of the others, who clapped their hands in approval. He required the right to put a question, whatever it was. Captivated, if more or less anxious, all agreed.

He took his viol and after a sweet enough prelude led up to what he was going to ask by recalling that after the struggles against the Saracens, thanks to the accords at that time made with them, the use of Turkish baths had expanded, and at the same time the fashion of depilation. Then he sang:

Lady, answer me if you dare
How much hair you have
You know where?

A great lifting of shoulders, then a laugh from everyone, so inordinate with some of them as to shake their breasts almost out of their corsage. The beauty, not divining what he wanted to come of it, even though troubled, replied simply:

"Know that there is none."

Then he sang out loud, with a cheerful air, brutally,

I well believe you, for a path
That is well trodden grows no grass!

This time some breasts fell right out, such was the laughter, double what it was before, for all knew her to be very flirtatious. As for her, all composure lost, their laughter sent her on her way. Her face as red as her dress, or almost so, she walked straight out into the gardens. Not even hearing the bird song or bursts of song from the other tents; not even seeing the primroses, daffodils, and tulips that bloomed in the great flowerbeds against the walls, or the tender pink petals of the peach tree blossom; or the yellow broom and white hawthorn that flecked the hedges alongside the forest edge. All weighed heavily upon her in her distress.

Part of her life that she supposed unknown had been revealed nakedly to all. Well, one thing was for certain, she was not in disgrace for nothing – for she always took a chance at adventure.

As quickly as she had gone, she now decided to return, feeling alone near the forest and slightly frightened as evening fell. She reproached herself, resolved to return to a world of new faces, and was calmed to hear a voice nearby singing:

It is an honour my true love to serve
And from a sweet lady thus to deserve
A place in her bed, and there to be
Naked as needles and face to face
The better to fondle and to embrace
And give thanks to her as she does to me.

Smiling, she thought to herself that she had done well in this respect, and in good taste, and would do so again, as often as she could. For nothing, no nothing, was worth more. At this vision and reassured hope, her chagrin vanished and she regained her natural charm and lightness of heart as if nothing had happened.

A clerk was seated under a great oak and reading on his knees by the light of three torches *The Art of Love* by André the Chaplain, which explained, in detail, legitimate reasons for the natural act. It said that the authority of Love and his Parliaments held by the ladies was in accord with an obligation to devote one's life to an ideal of beauty, the cult of the saints, honesty before God, and respect of the faeries in the woods. This was opposed to the cruel demands of heredity in marriages, and matrimonial claustration.

It showed the need for free choice of lovers each for each – creating quite naturally a true, noble, gentle and superior secret order. A sweet framework foiled by these strict and savage brutal times that no longer responded to reality.

It praised the ladies for the disarming power of their calming and divine hands, linked with those of loyal and fervent friends against abuse, violence, and all possession that calls itself obligatory, which is without love and governed by cupidity.

And the clerk noted article XXVI of the *Art of Love*:

Amor nihil posset leviter amori denegari. "Love denies nothing to love."

X

Wedding Night

The Countess of Poitiers and her daughter, with their ladies in waiting, had accompanied Melusine and her slow undressing, all talking about the duties of a bride. After marvelling at her robe, they admired her lingerie, then her figure, more beautiful than ever in the midst of the discarded finery from which she emerged as if reborn, new, bright, nearly naked, like the goddess Aphrodite from the waves of the sea.

"Whatever we do, society is built in such a way that, although we know how to have the last word ourselves, we must let our lord think he is the stronger. Do so with yours," counselled the Countess, "and remain loving so that no other tries to divert him, especially in your court."

"So it is, and so it will remain," replied Melusine, who knew her own power.

And the daughter of the Countess admired her assurance, thinking no one could ever know, or love, a more beautiful lady.

"All must depend on us," she whispered, without really knowing what she was saying, but thinking it sounded more profound by sighing.

"That all depends," protested a lady who for a long time had lost her youth and sighed in regret rather than admiration.

Then, sententiously, for she belonged to a Court of Love, where she thought herself a canoness of good counsel, even though she had never attained the beauty of Ermengarde of Narbonne, she recalled the lay of the Trot, where the knight Norois saw a squadron of faithful and glorious lovers pass before his eyes, riding brightly caparisoned horses; then one of fickle lovers spurring raw boned nags whose trot shook their backs and breasts and broke their teeth; while she waited complacently for the thin and dried black hunters.

But Melusine: "At least they were not feeble, ill or perverse. Evil never comes from two hearts that love each other. Now, I am sure of ours, knowing mine, for one thing, and having judged my lord's on the other, and not from the outside. I do not believe men or women who are jealous have true happiness; their ill intentions rebound on themselves, lost by excess. But I know none of those, for the moment, among those invited to our wedding; and I am completely happy."

"Completely?" asked the Countess Blanche.

Melusine smiled.

"It comes, it goes, but always there if either one seeks it."

And as they finished warming the half open bed, she stretched out within it.

Raymondin had no wish to wait, and no one tried to delay him. As he arrived at the threshold the ladies greeted him with laughing faces, wished him well and a long wedding night as they pulled the curtains of the bed around them. Then they retired quietly and closed the door. But Raymondin looked out of the curtains to make sure that they were alone. Then, the others having gone, the two of them, rediscovering the happiness of their first time of coming together, lost themselves one within the other, until exhausted, at dawn.

That night, they say, the valiant Urian was conceived, who became King of Cyprus.

XI

The Court of Love

It was perhaps a little late when Raymondin rejoined his guests in the morning as they waited patiently to celebrate mass, for he had much to thank God for, with all his pleasures and prosperity.

Celebrations went on for a fortnight. The gifts were as rich as the feasts: all the ladies received jewels, all the knights arms. The Countess of Poitiers already wore an engraved golden clasp on which Bishop Hilarion, the first pioneer of the faith at Poitiers, held up his hand above his meditative head in blessing. Her daughter Blanche had a bonnet finely worked with pearls alternating with sapphires and emeralds. Rather than a weapon, the Count of Forez had been given a cup, so beautifully worked that he was looking at it on all sides when Raymondin surprised him in his examination and whispered:

"When you get home, brother, drink from it thinking of the love of my wife and me, and the good wine of confidence and abandon. It is that which brings happiness, believe me. And to the wise and brave who live their lives in faith with no need for self reproach. May God protect them, above all when the Enemy is lurking. As for others, may leprosy smite them!"

Count Bertrand, hearing these remarks, approved, took the cup himself and turned it in the sunlight. It was of polished silver and gold, so cunningly worked that where the metals rejoined after their interlacing one could not say whether it had been formed from one metal or not. It recalled to mind a chalice, although rounder, shorter, less high – a little even in the form of the Graal. And no doubt to make it better remembered, along its stem and circular base, rubies alternated with sparkling garnets. When he had examined it well, he raised it the length of his arms as if to offer it to the sun, that was mirrored in its metal and its gems. Then he returned it to the Count of Forez declaring that it was a cup of Good Faith.

On Saturday the games were particularly lively. There were so many jugglers, jongleurs, trouvères and story tellers under the elm that no-one noticed the absence of Melusine that evening, apart from Raymondin's brother.

"Where is your wife then?" he asked.

"She is resting."

He chuckled, but without pressing the matter, so as not to question quite openly if this was quite natural.

Raymondin, annoyed, could not resist the rejoinder, "You have not yet imbibed the spirit of your cup. It was not made just to be an ornament. Have you used it?"

"Not yet, but don't worry, I quite like it."

Then he added:

"Is it enchanted, to cast spells on those who drink from it?"

"That depends on you. But if its origin interests you, it is the work of a goldsmith who works here in Poitiers, near St John's baptistery, and was chosen as the best of all he had. As long as it pleases you, you will always find in it what I have already said – and the memory of my affection."

Embarrassed, his brother embraced him, and they spoke of other things.

Their walk led them towards a great tent where a Court of Love had just concluded – a tribunal of ladies and lords in the company of trouvères commenting, in the light of André the Chaplain, on a book by the Monk of the Golden Isles – a very enlightened religious – based on the works of another, the famous Hermentaire. To validate the rulings just rendered, a clerk recited the origins of the Code of Love.

This is what he was saying:

"Ladies and knights, maidens and squires, know that it came from Brittany in ancient times. A recognised miracle brought us these leaves of gold which affect the highest ideals of the human heart. For all that is great has a mysterious origin, a legendary birth. This Book of Books – after the Holy Bible – remained for centuries at the court of King Arthur, in the talons of a great hawk, retained by a charm reputed to be invincible. A black knight who had never been seen before, as unknown as his sombre armour, won it. Nothing could resist him. Not even the magic castle in the thick of Broceliande, at a place where the fir trees are so thick and close together that only the strongest man can pass, or the most thin, worming his way through so many trunks as to lose his way, ceaselessly repeating his tracks by going round in circles. Not the draw bridges of the seven walls, one after the other, of the castle that stood on a hill in a great clearing. Not the regular and perfect perch at the centre where the hawk lived, its body immobile, but beating its wings in an enchanted ritual. Once arrived there, would you like to know how he succeeded?"

"Yes! Yes!" pressed a hundred voices.

"Hear then the fine story of prowess and love. The knight was walking his palfrey through the depths of the royal forest, sprightly and smart, passing where none had been able to go before him, dreaming of the conquest that none had achieved, but where many had left their bones, which for some time he found whitening on his way. They simply reminded him of a childhood story, that of Tom Thumb. Then he saw, riding on a hack, an astonishing maiden of supple grace and striking beauty whose hair floated loose in the wind. He stopped, and she also.

They saluted each other courteously.

'I do not know what you are looking for, my fine Black Prince, but be sure that without my help you will never find it.'

'My beauty, if you want me to believe you, you must know the reason for my journey, my vigil and its destiny. So tell me.'

The beautiful maiden said:

'The lady who holds your love has imposed upon you the task of conquering the hawk that watches on its golden perch in the portico of the court of Arthur, the sovereign king.'

'That is true.'

'Learn then, as prize for your candour, that you cannot obtain the wondrous book from the bird described by your lady without proving, by force of arms against all the knights of King Arthur, that she whose colours you wear under your black armour is superior in beauty to all others. And that is not all. You will cross the fatal threshold only if you can show to those who ceaselessly guard it the magic glove to which the bird will willingly come. As for the glove itself, that is only obtained by triumphing over the two most formidable champions in Christendom.'

It seemed to the knight that the maiden did not reveal all these things to him without good reason and with an eye to a favourable future, and that new times were about to dawn. Like today, it was a clear golden April where all widely welcomed him. The grass was green and fresh. The flowers opened, happy in their colours. The air itself was a caressing breeze. All promises affirmed for certain.

Raising his visor, the knight dismounted, knelt before the beautiful maiden and vowed that he could not, and would not, refuse her aid. Then, on his feet, declared he would humbly submit to her rule, as well as receiving her permission to make known the superiority of his lady.

'If you say yes to my two prayers,' he concluded, 'I am sure I can meet all without fear.'

Impressed by such modesty and audacity so well combined, the Faery of the Forest, for it was she, decided to help him, and rendered her lips to him. He raised his helmet, and quite overcome, but calmly, received from her the kiss of comfort, agreement and protection.

'Now take my horse,' she said to him, 'it is yours. It knows all the secrets of the bushes and trees of Broceliande. With him you can pass the thickest forest.'

At the same time she gave her new friend all the passwords, taught him how to respond to questions, along with the best advice, warning him of circumstances where he must omit nothing he had learned. Having left nothing to chance, reassured by the attention he gave as a guarantee of his memory, she finished by commending him above all not to forget, once his victory was attained over the guardians of the magic glove, to take it from the column of gold where it was suspended.

'The glove does all, or very nearly so, fine sir. It is the absolute talisman. Without it, courage, cold blood, prudence will serve for nothing.'

She kissed him again, mounted his horse, waved her hand in farewell and disappeared.

He set forth on the steed she had given him, rapid, light, energetic, that took the place of his own. With the reins held loosely in his hand, he let it lead him. Thus he came, as he would not otherwise have done, to the country of his adventures and tests."

Here the clerk stopped a moment, and resumed.

"Maidens and knights, ladies and squires, you are not paying enough attention. So I will tell you briefly that the events were many, that the black knight passed all the obstacles, and came to the end of his perils. After all that, he removed the magic glove from a golden column that supported the weight of the palace. Then having triumphed over this last enchantment, when he appeared before the portico of the famous perch the hawk flew up and landed on his gloved fist. Attached to its spurs was the Book of Books (after the Evangelists) with the golden leaves.

He hesitated to look at the marvellous manuscript but a distant voice reassured him.

'Thou who hast known how to take the pages of honey from the peaceful hawk, take them: the rules engraved upon them have been inscribed by the King of Love himself, to be venerated and taken to heart by all true lovers.'

In obedience, the lover, whom the hawk on his fist had fixed with its small golden clear piercing eyes, detached the unique book, and as the bird flew to the heights of the sky, felt himself transported too.

In an instant, no more time than it took for the hawk to beat its wings, or open and close its strange eyes, he found himself back in the forest at the place where he had met the lovely maiden with the beautiful hair. She did not conceal the pleasure that they both shared.

'Go in joy, valiant knight, dear friend; Blue Brittany awaits your return. Do not be sad to leave me so soon. Wherever you are, near or far, happy or unhappy, you have only to think of me if you want me, and I will come quickly to be near to you.'

They embraced again, for a long time.

Then he returned to his lady and mistress, who called a feast and recompensed him in every way. Then she convoked the first Court of Love.

When she had finished holding the numerous plenary meetings, all went their ways swearing to practise and to spread the rules that had been written by a god on the golden leaves of the mysterious manuscript. So that despite bad masters lacking true wisdom, all peoples on the face of the earth should come, little by little, to form the republic of lovers."

The discussion continued, but as the two articles to discuss were the first and the thirty-first, Raymondin, in his present certainty, which sufficed him, went off with his brother, who took his revenge by counselling him in his turn to drink from the cup of faith.

These articles were – and remain what they were then:

I – Causa conjugii non est ab amore excusatio.
"Marriage is no excuse for not loving."

XXXI – Unam feminam nihil prohibet a duobus amari, et a duabus mulieribus unum.
"Nothing forbids a woman from being loved by two men, or a man by two women."

·XII·
Questions After the Feast

The feasting complete, Raymondin took care to accompany the long line of departing guests, leading the way with the Count of Forez and the Count of Poitiers.

They talked of the recent happy days together, with particular memories of the events that had most diverted them. All three were in the greatest natural gaiety until Bertrand, curious about what he had discussed several times with his mother regarding Raymondin's marriage, became once more indiscreet.

"Cousin, a question comes to my lips that has occupied me much, and proves my affection, for it is not enough simply to love those of whom one is fond, but to be assured as to the reasons for their happiness. This time, open up, since the deed is done and cannot be undone. I would very much like to know the lineage of your wife. We know only her name, her grace and her generosity, which are unequalled. This is fine, but it does not dispense with the rest."

To which the Count of Forez added, "So my brother, you see that I am not the only one to be worried. You do not realise that these questions are also ceaselessly mine, and my anxiety is not allayed by the fact that you will not, or cannot, answer them. Of your wife, all that is known is the name of a far kingdom that is said to be hers and she the issue of noble blood, but that is only, after all, conjecture."

Bitten to the heart, Raymond would have liked to spur his mare through the forest and fly from them, at the same time wishing them prey to the forks of devils. But he continued at the same pace and replied calmly:

"You ask me, my friends, to divulge a secret that does not belong to me, that is not mine. If I should reveal to it to anyone it would certainly be to you Sir. And the same to you, my brother," he said in a less formal voice, turning toward the Count of Forez. "But I must keep it to myself. Hence the secrecy. All I can say about it is what you already know or have sensed for yourselves. That Melusine has never been brought up in rudeness, or poverty, nor without what we all take for granted in our own lives. All about her, I tell you, is noble – all! She is fortunate not to need to know the extent of all her resources, a concern for which is in many cases despicable or secondary. She has been brought up to be an example in dignity to the most proud.

"As to your worries, trust in my vigilance, few of them are likely. As for sincerity, so for the heart. I therefore ask you, as lords and as friends, to query no more. I avow to that which counts. Whatever she is – she pleases me. She is my lady and my love, and placed above all things, for the love that I have for her, and owe her. And because she is to me what I am to her. I do not know how to speak otherwise. To doubt her would be unworthy of me, and more than it would be for you. Stupid, odious or foolish I may be, but whether suspicions come from you or myself, they poison the springs of happiness."

Both were forced to understand his tone as well as his words.

"It is enough, Raymondin," said the Count of Poitiers. "Since you have such prodigious – and honourable – confidence in her, we cannot fail to have it ourselves. Your own, and our affection for you, obliges us in that. So be assured, once and for all, that we equally honour and accept your wife, as our cousin and as a lady, on your word, of noble extraction."

"I say the same, my brother. What you say is enough for me and I will not seek further, in the faith of a relative who loves you, and seeks to know no more of it."

And the journey continued.

When they had left, Raymondin, hard put to contain himself, spurred back towards the Fountain of Thirst, no longer in the same frame of mind as when he had left. All that he had not wanted to think about since he had met Melusine bore down upon him like an increasingly heavy weight until he felt he could no longer bear it – relieved only by the memory of the physical joys they had shared together, and towards which he galloped the more quickly as he recalled them. But still his mind returned to those detested questions that tormented him.

The forest, in which – at a stroke one night – the stars of his destiny had shone so brightly, suddenly turned hostile. He recalled the recent night journey when they had seen the eyes of wolves gleaming, somewhat dreading them, and when the little green page had killed one of them with a single arrow. What could he do to draw a bead on a menace he felt rising before him like a beast, only more dangerous because it was invisible!

Then, as he heard a strange movement in a nearby ditch he recalled the fatal hunt, the implacable enemy, the light and deadly spear in his hand, the dead boar stretched out on Count Aimery, and the strange fate to which he owed all that had since happened to him, that now weighed on him like a nightmare. His burning head gave birth to the worst anxieties. The solitude of Colombier increased his distress as he began to ask himself if he had not aided Fate to lead him on, in turn, to his own death.

The more he yielded to this vague anguish, the less he felt at ease, for he felt it could only increase in the future. He needed to define it if he could not resolve it, and it took, in his fevered imagination, the appearance of a winged sphinx in constant movement, beating membranous wings in an atmosphere of damp fog in which her lower body was obscured. Astonished at his ignorance of what this posed vision meant, without a definition of its nature or reality, or what it fearsomely implied, he told himself that only he could take it upon himself to discover; not those whose affection, curiosity or jealousy had only called on him the need to do so.

The need to know became the focus of his very being, his life, his situation. All now appeared to be instable and too uncertain to be maintained. His future was at the mercy of a nothing, of an indiscretion, of a whim. Tortured by this, he decided he must question Melusine, if only for himself, for himself alone.

But was that not, exactly, just what his oath prevented? Impossible to doubt that. So what to do?

With his sharp spurs, his mail clad legs in supple steel, his long pointed shoes weighing light in the slim stirrups, he roused his chestnut mare and galloped hell for leather through the forest of buzzing insects and singing birds. Then, at a stroke, in a moment, all was strangely silent, as if the increased speed of his course snatched away all that had obsessed him. He even began to ask himself where reality began.

Had he not fallen prey to a moment of weakness, a sort of vertigo? What represents absolute certainty? That which is seen as happiness, the experience a satisfied expansion of being, is not that the best, in fact the true, the more real, at least the most adequate?

Can a truth that destroys everything really be a truth? Or, on the other hand, does it prove by this that it *is* a truth? Illusion or not, is not the one who makes it real and at the same time the most favourable the best? It may not be true from a certain point of view of cold quintessential abstraction, but nothing is worth more than the reality that comes from it when this realisation is happiness. Above all, is it not a question, contrary to the advice of the piss-colds and the pernickety, of being happy? He had suffered too much not to convince himself of it. In order to get there truly he had to persevere rather than give up. Since God, through his clergy, had blessed it, why be concerned? Would it not even be sinful to go back on all that? Deadly to seek in the beyond, wanting to see further than the beautiful and good blessings that came from her grace? Senseless pride, luciferian, to dwell on it? A crime to doubt that which he had only to believe? In fact, was it not the gift of Providence? And the more it showed itself to be marvellous, the more it proved, irrefutably, that it came from that.

In light of this new reasoning, composed like the former, but opposed to it, he gradually recovered his calm, peace and equilibrium. That which he imagined earlier was at the instigation of his Lord and of his brother, for he began to doubt that he had ever really thought it. They might have done so, but not even them, for what is more, he excused them now to the point of forgiving them for what appeared to be an oblique attack of the Devil. After a minute, he was so certain of this that he made the sign of the cross, so as to banish it, and felt better, at ease with himself and with everything different. Dreaming of the Fountain of Thirst, he was sure that the water of Truth flowed from there. And the closer he approached, he already breathed in the air, by the arousal of his desire, the invisible presence of Melusine.

Finally, had he not sworn never to ask her about this mystery? So best not to think of it. For was it not that to which he owed all? Had become his life? His sweating mare had slowed down and he let her go at a walk the better to anticipate more sweetly the joy of recovering what was not only given, but freely offered to him, by the most beautiful woman that he had ever known, and who was now his very life. Of the idea that he could lose her, and by his own fault, nothing remained. And free from these former bad thoughts he began once more to be full of happiness. The long golden body of his lady stretched out with her arms behind her head, with its three sweet darker shadows, and her hair beneath her reaching down to her knees under the sheets, appeared before him with a precision and an insistence that raised him to the summit of desire. Nor did it seem possible that this perfect vision came only from himself; he imagined it all round, and convinced himself that she thought of him with an equal longing at the same time. An irresistible haste to rejoin her seized him to urge on his mare, without pity of her fatigue, with great blows of the spurs and an imperious sureness of hand.

Bathed in sunlight, the forest lived with him, at one with his senses, his young blood and his dreams. The branches brushed against him with suggestive promises, as if they were the female servants of Melusine, their empress and their faery. They were fine and sweet with their first little silky leaves, caressing his face like her hair, and some, where the buds still held in the stalk, like long thin fondling fingers. All the legends that the harpers tell came back to him in waves of melody, borne by the wind of the woods and the speed of his passing. Above all, the most touching, from his adolescence, that had impressed their enchanted arabesques on his memory at an age when the opening awareness of the world is still like virgin wax. All the music of verse and song, attended by the beating wings of happiness, bringing a sense of certainty of the invisible in which, as a good Christian, he already naturally believed. Amongst others, he recalled the strophes of the old bard Hélinard when he told of ancient druids truly approaching the faeries in the same way as the women saints, of whom, he assured, they had been the initiators. Melusine no doubt had them among her ancestors. She had both. All thus became possible, natural and good. They lived one and all thanks to that, in mastering life, which is the best way to live it, because one abandons the unfortunate in the best possible way, and possesses, in the best possible way too, the excellent. Today is better than yesterday, which is no more. And of tomorrow, which is yet to be, one does not know the outcome.

Thus, he arrived.

And here he was astonished once again, for at the Fountain of Thirst he found the feast still as lively as when he had left, as if it had never come to an end, but was simply occupied by new faces.

As the whole court of knights came to salute him, Melusine appeared, and as she respectfully kissed his forehead before everyone, found the means to whisper in his ear more tender proposals, and then announced:

"My dear lord, here are your barons, come to swear allegiance to you."

They were magnificent, armed in great and beautiful style. A great hauberk covered the body from neck to knees, the sleeves reaching to the wrists. An embroidered robe down to the feet covered the padded gambaison. The helmet, pointed at the top, was a little curved at the front, and rested on a pad of rich material that passed over the mail hood. Each carried a great almond shaped shield, almost five feet long, and when they turned it, one could see its iron central boss with its system of straps ornamented with gold embroidery, and a long belt that allowed it to be hung round the neck. Each shield, painted from top to bottom, carried a different device, in long letters, at the top; the centre was occupied with a coat of arms or animal head; the bottom plain or painted with parallel bars, lengthways, in two colours. At the neck was an ivory horn on a short silk cord. The sword was long and heavy, sharpened both sides, the point a little rounded, made to thrust or slash. The guard was a simple cross with a strong hilt at its base, tapered slightly towards the pommel in the form of a vertical disc, surmounted with a metal button. They wore it attached to a baldric of which each end, split into strips, formed a leather ring under the cape, and thence to a belt, so that its end fell back on the stomach, and its boxwood scabbard was covered with a wild beast's skin. One of the barons, the oldest, who seemed in command of the others, displayed on his shield a sort of crouching winged siren whose arms held an anchor. Raymondin could not recall ever having seen such arms before, and could not interpret the meaning of the heraldic language.

Once Melusine and he were alone, they embraced, in all ways and for a long time, for that is what pressed upon them most. Then she made him tell her of his journey.

She was well pleased at his cool and wise response to the questions of the Count of Poitiers and the Count of Forez, and said: "All will always be well as long as you act like that. Do not give way. Shut yourself away if need be. Risk battle and danger rather than talk about it. For if you fail in that, we will both of us be lost."

·XIII·

Life At Lusignan

And so they lived happily together for a long time.

The tents and temporary installations of the feast having been struck, a veritable inundation of stones of all sizes encompassed the rocks of the Fountain of Thirst, accompanied by numberless workers, coming on foot, on horseback or in long wagons strangely shaped like ships such as were unknown in the country. Thus the famous and formidable castle grew as a haven for their love. There was no one who had not heard of it. There existed no stronger or more beautiful a fortress, even at Coucy much later, as this one of Lusignan.

The immense army of workers was directed by a mysterious architect whom all obeyed without a murmur, as if his genius and his will were recognised and accepted by all. A singular spontaneous discipline kept each in his place and created a harmony as flawless as their order and their methods. The master, present throughout, vigilant and active, taciturn and calm, with a pale impassive face framed by a black beard, his hair under a turban-like head dress, seemed the scion of some unknown eastern country.

Under his direction the castle grew quickly on the great rock, which seemed as if it had been made for it. The central keep, high and narrow, of extraordinary strength and solidity through the thickness of its walls, rose like a towering spire from the fortress itself, its walls yet thicker, with crenelations and machicolations adapted to the needs of war, and dominated by a high watchtower. As implacable were the other buildings, and the walls that one after the other defended the approach, each accompanied by impassable ditches, of which the first ones, counting from the outside, and the two before last, were six feet deep and twenty wide, while the last, like that of the keep itself, was thirty feet wide, with a moat twice as deep, on the dark waters of which swam black and white swans. The strong machicolated towers within its seven walls had small, narrow windows, slanted so as to complement and aid neighbouring towers under assault. One did not know what most to admire, the art and science of defence realised in this powerful ensemble, or the beautiful proportions that emerged from it. Those who had specialised in this form of work in the county of Poitiers, father and son, swore they had never seen the like. They looked for faults at every stage, but found no part to criticise, and admired how all the stones were cemented together without even showing the joins.

As an outer defence, a bank of earth stretched a long way, first at a gentle slope, then almost perpendicular, so that none could scale it without being subject to blows. It descended towards the forest in a great space of meadow, at the centre of which stretched an oval lake whose source was within the lake itself, and filled all the ditches between the walls. The embankment was reinforced with enormous chamfered stones from which jutted monstrous thick planks with sharp iron spikes to the fore. At the bottom, before the ditches, were hidden traps concealed by bushes. And under the first trees near by, further terracing, marvellous to behold, overlooked the north and south sides of the road to Lusignan.

The castle itself was like an immense oval, a little broader in the centre than at the ends, of which the higher, from a little further away, appeared slightly wider. Its regular alignments, its vertical walls, at one with the rock, were used to double advantage; being so high, virtually inaccessible, with long crenelations and towers, and here and there its barbicans.

Its terracing down to the plain and the wood, from the very first contact, and increasingly, could only discourage an assailant. It was not just that all up to the forest all around was redoubtable, but the fact that it was also deceptive. If the first wall was taken, the extensive clearing could be flooded by the lake. There was thus no attack or even investment that could be prepared by surprise.

What is more, in the forest, under certain impenetrable thickets, underground tunnels emerged at different places. These were known only to the masters, the men employed at this work dying almost as soon as it was finished, without anyone knowing why or how, for their end appeared to be quite natural. In case the entrances were discovered, beyond two iron portcullises, that only negotiation of the wall permitted to be worked, a man-trap followed, and a ditch full of water at which one had to stop before going further. Contained in the thickness of the wall under tufts of ivy was an iron ring, which pulled strongly, caused planks of wood to form a bridge that allowed one to pass. An identical arrangement existed on each side, so in case of emergency the whole space of the ditch could be covered to give passage to a troop of men.

The most extensive of these underground tunnels forked halfway down, leading to different places at the edge of the forest of Colombier. The one that led towards Poitiers, after another fork, came out half a league from the first, in two little copses spaced in the fields about a double crossbow shot one from the other.

When all was done, the architect left as he had come, with his thousands of workmen, without even, as far as Raymondin knew, asking for payment.

One morning, in fact, on walking out on the walls, Raymondin saw none of them, but all had been replaced by as many men at arms. And as it seemed that their duties were well organised, Raymondin, who was getting used to all this, questioned no one and indeed felt no longer much surprise. All appeared so natural that he neither thought any more of it or spoke about it to his wife.

Another care concerned her, being confined in childbed, and for nothing in the world did he want to disturb her. And so it was at Lusignan that Melusine brought her first child into the world. A boy, who was much welcome, but also disfigured, for he had a short and wide face in which one eye was red and the other green; and as he grew up, his ears grew out of proportion until they resembled the handles on a basket.

He was baptised with the name Urian, as we have already noted in telling of his parents' wedding night when he was conceived. He was particularly cherished and his deformities in no way hindered their tenderness toward him.

Melusine however, as time passed, noticed how each Saturday a dark shadow would come over the face of her husband. And on that day he would spend longer with his son, teaching or playing with him, asking roundabout questions, as if he believed it possible to obtain from him, either through his innocence or some unknown quality, what he could never learn from her. Or at least some indication of a hidden clue that might take him there. But as it never came, he would sit with the child on his knees, gazing at him for a long time.

A few months later, in the early hours one morning, when they were in a loving embrace, for an embrace, whilst usually expressing passion, can sometimes cover something more pressing, Melusine whispered:

"Sweetheart, I have been thinking of your interests and of your glory, rather than my own. And an idea has come to me that may appeal to you, as you have always taken heed of me. Our future does not belong to ourselves alone. We must think of our children – for everything tells me that we shall have more – and especially their inheritance. Part of what should be theirs ought already to have been returned to you, for you and your brother have been defrauded. The borders and country of the Guerande are rightfully yours, Penicens as well. If you go there and appeal to the King of Brittany he will receive you straight away."

He was glad that she had included his brother in this enterprise, from whom some ill feeling had come. And he wondered at her knowledge of these rumours, of which he had heard much spoken, but had not thought about for some time. As his eyes could not hide his thoughts, Melusine continued:

"The father of you both once quarrelled with the old king's nephew and killed him. Not daring to stay in Brittany he went off on adventure until the day he married the sister of the Count of Poitiers, your uncle. Have no doubt about it. What I tell you is true. And if the present king does not wish to receive you or Forez, do not be angry. For believe me, he will come round to it in time."

At the thought of leaving the dear creature who had brought him so much happiness he was tempted to ignore such old dreams and stick to life as it was. On the other hand, as she well knew, he was accustomed to obey her. And all indicated, anyway, that she was right. He was delayed at first, however, by the need to inform Forez, and put off a final decision until he heard from him.

The response was not long in coming, and was negative through embarrassment. It was said that his brother, whilst rejoicing at his departure, feared it, for reasons he did not explain. Feelings of members of a family one against the other are rarely disinterested, and can come more from calculation than from the heart. Those who do not realise this are ever the dupes of the others.

No doubt awareness of these lamentable things was why Our Lord, although he pardoned them (as he forgave all except hatred and sacerdotal pride) told his disciples, in certain cases, to leave their families. For though he took care to respect the independence of each one, he understood that if this independence was to be real, it must come from a freedom nourished by judgement and feelings, without which the world, even one so well organised as the Roman empire, could not exist.

He developed this ideal in each one, knowing in advance that the little country where his cross would stand would serve to unite East and West. And the kingdom of France would be, through its knights, a true and sweet nation with the finest swords and most agreeable women, if the essence of his doctrine was on their lips and in their souls, like the hilts of their fine swords, that were in the form of his cross. But those who spoke in the name of the Nazarene misunderstood his true nature for most of the time – if not all the time. And the Count of Forez was one of these.

"My love, you are every day more dear to me," Raymondin said, "and I shall suffer greatly to leave you, but you know I would never refuse you anything. There is nothing to the world I would not do to please you, and I know you always strive for our greater good. So I will go and seek out the king of Brittany."

She prepared him with excellent advice, and as he committed it to memory he admired such practical detail, precise, subtle, maternal, that told him not only of things but about people, their possibilities, their strengths and weaknesses, with foreknowledge of their character and probable secrets. She finished by saying:

"Go bravely, and although it is needless to say, for I know your bravery, never, at any time, fear anything, neither persons, nor things that may occur. God will help you in all you undertake, as long as you are just and true. And I know that with you it cannot be otherwise. If you are ever weak or tired or in doubt in the face of danger, think of me, for my thoughts will never cease to watch over you like little votive lamps."

On the eve of his departure, she gave him his spurs, which were of gold, and his sword, which she had prepared in secret, knowing his tastes so well as to make him true to her for the rest of his life. She had placed it, for the last two months, on the altar of the chapel of Our Lady of Thirst where their marriage had been celebrated, so it was blessed by the deacon when he celebrated the Mass each day. Thus sanctified, she had baptised it with the name of Martha, she who tended the household and the fireside, not daring to give it her own, although she secretly asked pardon of the saint to allow another name, that of Melusine, to be connected to the noble arm and the lips of the only man she would ever love.

The sword was splendid, with its curved quillons widening in tempered steel, and silver embossed with gold. A masterpiece of ornamental enamelling showed unicorns the length of its hilt. Perhaps most astonishing was the quality of its steel, into which nothing could bite, tempered in a way of which the modern world has lost the secret. The blade was double ridged each side, with a large central groove down two thirds of its length.

It was more beautiful even than that of Hermann de Salza, grandmaster of the Teutonic Knights from 1200 to 1239, which until 1917 was to be found in the Hermitage Museum at St Petersburg and which perhaps still waits there until the day of the Last Judgement.

Raymondin in Brittany

ere we can do no better than tell Raymondin's adventures in Brittany as they have been recorded by a bard whose name has been lost to us but who is of the little known school of Barzaz-Breiz. However, his contemporaries called him after the name of the little village where he was born – Penhoel. And they still spoke of him in the time of the great story teller Mathurin the Blind.

HERE BEGINS THE STORY OF THE BARD OF PENHOEL
As the high, and sometimes very high, ground began, covered with daffodils and broom, Raymondin and his escort realised they had entered that country of countries which is at one with the sea, which all but dominates it, as its name Armorica reveals (Ar – of ; Mor – the sea). But apart from their first sight of Blue Brittany, the charming and moving popular songs they heard left them in no doubt. Workmen on the roads carried cow skin flagons on their shoulders or long gourds full of cider. When they stopped they had a bowl of onion soup with a hunk of bread. The escort, what is more, met a fair number of walkers, including pilgrims, for they were far from "the Kalangoan" – the first days of winter – and above all, in the hollows of small valleys or on the tops of hills, in tiny chapels with bulging naves, some with ceilings emblazoned with golden stoats, where a squat country pilgrim might be seen, hallowed, leaning on a long staff, sometimes curved at the end like a bishop's crozier.

The men at arms of the prince of Lusignan caused something of a stir in quiet Brittany, being a fine strong party of 300 knights and squires, each one wearing a long tunic with wide sleeves, cut on each side at the bottom so as to fit well on horseback, along with 200 gentlemen, with mail shirt over a thick gambeson, complete with tail piece and leg harness. The pages carried lances and helmets, and all rode confidently on brightly caparisoned horses.

Warned of their coming, the King of Brittany sent two knights of great renown along with their men, who, salutes having been exchanged, asked the reason for such armed numbers.

Raymondin replied: "Good sirs, tell the King of Brittany that Raymondin of Lusignan, vassal and cousin of the Count of Poitiers,

Bertrand, son of Aimery, comes to his kingdom (that may God preserve) and the lands that comprise it, in search of justice under his royal jurisdiction."

"If that is so, then welcome! The king, our lord, will give you fair hearing. Quéméniguant, where he waits you, is 20 leagues away, and there you will find Alain de Léon, who will make you welcome."

They then departed to tell their Master.

As soon as he was informed, the King sent his two sons, Alain and Henri, to meet the 500 horsemen, and Alain, who was the oldest, offered their father's hospitality. The three of them seemed well pleased with each other, and seeing eye to eye, rode on together towards Quéméniguant, Raymondin between the two brothers.

As they drew near, a curious knight of his suite, who had gone on ahead, came back to tell Raymondin he had prepared their encampment in the plain, a little before the town. They continued on their way and soon the king himself came to meet them on the road. After the usual presentations and compliments, they entered the town, in the midst of great show and jubilation. The supper was enormous and they ate as much as they were able. Then, rising from table, Alain de Léon took his guest by the hand, led him to a nearby hall, and said:

"I am very glad at your coming. And if you noticed during the meal that I seemed to be staring at you, it was because of your incredible resemblance to my brother, who left Brittany some forty years ago. Do you know anything about him that leads to you coming to see me? A quarrel with the former king's nephew drove him into exile."

"As for me, I am overjoyed to hear your noble words, for which I thank you greatly. And I hope you will tell me the cause of the quarrel between your brother and the king's nephew, for I have come with no other purpose."

"Why do you take this upon yourself? You are no more than thirty years old and that of which I speak took place forty years ago. And all happened so suddenly that neither I, nor anyone else knew much about it. It was that sort of affair that could never be spoken about – to the point of changing the subject if it should ever come up in conversation. Yet you, a stranger to these parts, to which you say you have come for the first time, seem to have heard about it. Tell me, dear sir, how did you know?"

And the old man with the fine bearing and trimmed beard and coat embroidered with many coloured silks, smiled at Raymondin as he had during the long meal, who smiled back equally.

"Was there, in your brother's time, a man of great authority in the court, but, as happens so often, unworthy of it?"

"There was! Together with his son, who is a knight. He took my brother's inheritance."

"Was his name Josselin du Pont, and his son Olivier?"

"Exactly!" Alain de Léon was astounded. "By the body of Christ, tell me about it!"

It was a question that had worried him since that distant time when neither justice nor truth had been possible, and which, without it being at all his fault, had left him with a certain remorse.

"Speak! It is impossible that you know all this. How did you learn it?"

"Noble sir, ask me no more for the present. I can say nothing now because it will be more important if saved for later. I ask only that you accompany me, you and your son, to see what can be done at the royal court. Then I will reveal all and clearly declare the quarrel that needs to be satisfied. And then you will love your brother, after whom one of your sons is named, all the more!"

"My court is held at Nantes," said Alain de Léon. "Count on me."

Here, after stopping for a rest by means of a song, of which the lines of the refrain were "Breiz da virvikenn", accompanied by his bagpipe, being alone, his Breton pipes and oboe at his feet, the bard of Penhoel continued:

The Tuesday before Pentecost they left for Nantes and a beautiful castle of rough grey stone that seemed made of rocks and sea mist, set with windows, some green, some blue, and others the white of foam. It held within, like a heart of oak encrusted with silver flowers, the throne of the Breton king, said to be an exact copy of that of the legendary King Arthur in Avalon.

They stopped near the ramparts where their camp had been prepared, dressed in new clothes, polished their armour, and entered the town, accompanied by forty knights as sumptuously dressed as themselves.

Installed on his throne, flanked by his barons and with his court before him, with a long wide passage left between them, the king of the Bretons received his son Alain first and questioned him.

"You are acquainted with a knight of whom I have heard great marvels. Who is he? For none here know of him."

"In faith sire, I am as astonished as you in this matter but unable to enlighten you. We will soon know what he requires of us, for he has come here to tell us. And here he comes."

But Raymondin first approached the son of Alain de Léon to ask if Josselin du Pont was present.

"He *is* here," he replied, "I have seen him, and am sure I was not mistaken, for I see enough of him to know him well. I do not know whether he holds his inheritance wrongly."

But as he spoke Raymondin interrupted.

"Show him to me!"

"You see that old man, down there, next but one to my father, who keeps looking around him at all sides. Yes, the oldest evil doer in ten kingdoms. Beside him is his son Olivier, who is worthless."

"I will avenge you soon, I promise you!"

Raymondin left him and went toward the King, before whom he put one knee to the ground and announced in a loud voice:

"High and powerful sire, your court is said to be a fount of law and justice. I have come here in homage to throw myself upon it."

"Your confidence is well placed," replied the King, "so tell me why you have come to appeal to our law and justice?"

Silence fell even amongst the greatest chatterers and all eyes were fixed on the lord of Lusignan.

"Before answering, illustrious sire, master, sovereign, king of all Blue Brittany, I ask that you recognise my rights, whatever they may be. What I have to announce is all to your profit and also to your honour, for a king surrounded by unworthy courtiers would be a poor one."

Alain de Léon stiffened, but the king merely said: "I promise you full justice, even if it were against my own brother."

"Noble sire," Raymondin began, "your predecessor reigned powerfully and valiantly. I speak of a time when Josselin du Pont and Alain de Quéméniguant here present before you were young. The king of whom I speak had a handsome and noble young man for a nephew. And there was also then alive a baron, Henri de Léon, the brother of Alain de Quéméniguant."

Before Raymondin could continue or the king answer Josselin du Pont interrupted:

"That is right. The knight who speaks of him might well add that this Henri de Léon treasonously killed the king's nephew, your predecessor, and fled the country. Since when there has never been any news of him. Thus the king gave me his lands, of which he had proved unworthy."

"Sire," continued Raymondin in the same tone as before, "ask this knight if he speaks the plain and entire truth on this sorry tale. If he does not do so, I will make him. And as for news, I bring it."

Josselin du Pont, as Raymondin had foreseen, could hardly restrain his anger, but hid his resentment.

"Knight, have you come to this country to slander the living on behalf of the dead? Your insinuations will carry no effect, I warn you."

"Sire," continued Raymondin, without regard to this air of menace, "Henri de Léon was courteous and valiant, and both the king and his nephew loved him. But this mutual affection, and certain and disinterested loyalty, was exploited by some evil felons. They insinuated to the royal nephew that unless he did something about it, the inheritance of the fine country of Brittany would go instead to Henri de Léon. That letters patent had already been written, passed and confirmed with the great seal. Such lies, that he took for the truth, saddened and angered the anxious nephew, who became the prey of these evil lords. At their instigation and that of Josselin – whom I name – he agreed to take part in an ambush against the one he believed to be dangerous and crooked. They fell upon him as he walked in the woods reading his book of hours, as was his custom, for the silence of the forest pleased him and responded to his religious sentiments, the high alleys of the trees crossing their branches like the arches of a cathedral. Not knowing who attacked him, for being of clear conscience he had no enemies that he knew of, Henri de Léon defended himself strongly, as he had every right to do. Mad with rage, the king's nephew struck him in the thigh with his sword. Rightly furious, Henri wrestled the sword from his hands and struck him on the temple with the pommel. The nephew's light helmet, weak in this place, gave in under the powerful blow and fractured his head. The barons ran off, showing their lack of honour, abandoning the one whom they had brought to his end. Henri de Léon, wanting to identify his aggressor, and if need be get help for him, uttered a cry of horror on realising he had unknowingly killed his friend and his lord, the royal nephew. Desperately, he pondered long before deciding to hide and in the end to go far away, on adventure, in hope of forgetting such a frightful memory. When Josselin du Pont – whom I name once more – was certain he had gone, he took the body of the nephew to the king, and accused Henri de Léon of having killed him by treason.

"That, Sire, is the plain and entire truth, including the perfidious felon Josselin. I desire that this be recognised and to any who dare claim that I have lied, I present my gauntlet and cry my name. I know that they are here."

And throwing down his left gauntlet, that he held in his hand, with a slap at the feet of the traitor, he called out in a strong and ringing voice:

"I am the son of Henri de Léon, and in the name of my father I call on you to admit your crime!"

Josselin du Pont, pale and tense, looked at the gauntlet on the ground, while Alain and his brother embraced the accuser. The stillness was such, the attention of all so fixed, the silence so total that many, both men and women, could hear the beating of their own hearts. The surprise and silence continued while Josselin, immobile, failed to take up the challenge.

The king uttered the first word, to express the thoughts of those present.

"Josselin, have you become deaf? As for me, I recall the truth of the proverb: 'Old sins make new shame'. What? This knight brings strange atrocious news; all the more strange for you, accused of felony, of treason, of crime. And yet you stay silent! How can you? I can neither understand it or hear anyone explain it. Answer quickly, for your sake and for us all. Your honour needs words."

Josselin du Pont, forcing himself to laugh spitefully, neither stepping forward or taking up the gauntlet, replied quietly: "Sire, how can I make a case against such words? This stranger loves gossip and so he has gossiped. But I do not believe his lies."

"Disloyal and discourteous one," cried Raymondin indignantly, "the gossip will fall on your head!"

He turned to the king:

"Powerful and noble sire, I require that you grant me the right of combat against this felon. And he can bring, if he so wishes, his son Olivier and another of his close friends. I will fight all three of them before your whole court. Then we will see on which side is the Right."

"Son of Henri de Léon, I will do it," said the king. "This time Josselin, you must reply."

But it was Olivier who spoke.

"Sire, it appears that this knight believes in scaring the cranes to flight, but I will make him see the contrary. He has not earned what he thinks so easily. He accuses my father falsely. Do I even have need to say so? I will prove on him that he has lied in his teeth, and will choose another of my lineage also to fight."

"As long as I live," replied the king strongly, "I will never permit a single knight to fight two others for a single vassal in the same quarrel. Great shame and cowardice on you for even having thought of it. It hardly proves your father has a good case. You will fight alone against the son of Henri de Léon to whom I give the choice of the day of battle."

"Sire, the sooner the better," said Raymondin. "My harness is ready. May God render merit to the judgement you have made."

All admired the courage of this knight that nobody knew. As for old Alain de Léon, he seemed sad at the thought that he would risk losing such a fine nephew when he had just had the joy of finding him. His sons, who did not believe there was any danger, showed great joy and said to their new friend:

"Good cousin, go strongly into battle, for you and for us, both against this felon and his line. We will come triumphant in the end with the help of God and our right."

"Fine and dear sirs, take who will this battle for himself," replied Raymondin. "As for me, I hope to play my part and acquit myself to the satisfaction of all. In any case, I thank you for your proof of friendship, as the worthy sons of a worthy brother of my noble father."

At that moment, there was great tumult all around. Prudent and well advised, the king sent to close all the doors of the manor so that none could enter or leave, and placed well armed men at the threshold of each. Returning to the hall of council, he ordered that none be so hardy as to say another word about it.

"This is no small quarrel," he said gravely, "it is a question of life or eternal dishonour to one or the other party. I do not say to which, nor do I refuse the justice that has been asked of me. Olivier, you will defend your father from this accusation, will you not?"

Once it had been guaranteed the King continued:

"The lists are nearby and ready. The combat will take place tomorrow. Know that if you are beaten, you will be hanged, as will your father. Whilst the same applies to the adverse party who must choose his hostages. But first I will take your father."

Then Josselin du Pont was taken and led out by four knights charged to take him to prison. Then the king turned to the lord of Lusignan for his hostages, and immediately the two sons and a dozen knights offered themselves with a common voice.

"That is enough," said the king, "I make you quit of prison, because of the good opinion I have of you and your champion. I feel this young man would not have risked this enterprise if he had no intention of seeing it through to the end."

Here the bard of Penhoel stopped again and, on a plaintive, slow melody, chanted rather than sang, a song of Léaurnan which began as follows:

The first meeting of my love and I was on a Sunday
When she danced with me she gave me a thousand caresses
They had said at the sight that she was my mistress
That she was my mistress.

But the song having no connection with the tale being told, we will reveal no more of it and take up the story where its teller left off.

Next day the king and the barons appeared on the high scaffolds prepared around the lists.

Raymondin appeared, shield round his neck, his lance straight ahead, coat of mail under the surcoat, riding a great iron clad destrier. Respects having been paid all round he dismounted as adroitly as if he had not been armoured and sat waiting his adversary.

Olivier delayed. Then appeared on a richly caparisoned horse, followed by his father, dressed almost the same, on a grey horse.

The Holy Evangelists were brought, bound between two plates, enamelled blue and gold, except in the middle where, under a sphere of rock crystal, could be seen a fragment of the wood of the true Cross. One of the acolytes who brought it had already marked the page where the gospel of St John commences. The priest took it, and opened the book on the page written and painted with long close characters. After having kissed the Gospels and crossing himself, the priest, newly tonsured, with smooth black hair cut close and very regular, in a sober chasuble whereon the monogram of Christ was inscribed between the shoulders, blessed the two sides and the lists, then waited.

Raymondin approached, and with a gesture clear and wide, extended his hand and outstretched arm over the sacred text, and swore, with a ringing and assured voice that Josselin du Pont had truly committed the treason of which he was accused. Then he knelt and kissed the parchment.

Josselin du Pont swore almost without hesitation in his turn, but in kissing the Holy Gospels became flustered and tottered, causing the book to fall from the desk upon which it lay. So stumbled Judas Iscariot, despite his apparent assurance, at the moment he gave the kiss to his Saviour in order to betray. It was impossible for Josselin to accomplish that which the lord of Lusignan had done so naturally. Seeing this, his son could only swear feebly and half heartedly, his conscience shaken by what he had just witnessed.

The herald at arms advanced. He ordered that no one make any sign or say any word that one of the champions could see or hear. Each then quickly left his place, apart from Josselin, and the guards left the close field. Raymondin mounted his horse at the same time as Olivier and the herald cried out three times:

"Let go your horses and do your duty!"

They threw themselves immediately into the fray one against the other. Only, as Raymondin did not want to set about his adversary before making the sign of the Cross, he put the butt of his lance to ground and sat on the neck of his horse. Olivier judging the position favourable and wanting to profit from it, launched himself on his way, lance couched, and came upon Raymondin aiming to take him full in the chest. Raymondin, with uncommon strength, only bent his back, but the lance was broken and fell from his hands.

"Ah, felon!" he cried, "you show well where you come from! Like father, like son!"

Seizing the flail mace that hung from the arc of his saddle, and which had three well sharpened points, each five inches long, he struck his adversary a violent blow on his helmet, that broke like glass, even though well tempered. One of the points entered the visor and what remained of the helmet and revealed Olivier's face. Although surprised at the outcome, the son of Josselin du Pont was not unhorsed. Leaving his lance he took up his sword and appeared not to fear his enemy.

The combat became furious and terrible. Wounds appeared, though lightly, as the well tempered armour appeared to parry most of the blows. Not holding back any more, in haste to win, Raymondin turned with his horse, picked up his lance and charged at Olivier, who, to defend himself, made him run here and there after him, to tire his horse, until he decided to leave it to render better account. Thus the day advanced without profit to anyone.

Raymondin realised he had to finish it, at whatever cost. He abandoned the lance which had not caused enough damage, took up his redoubtable flail mace, and spurred forward. At the first blow, Olivier du Pont's horse was struck on the forehead with such force that its steel head armour pierced its skin and the beast was knocked back on its haunches. Profiting from this, Raymondin took up what remained of his lance and struck Olivier in the body so hard that the iron entered the flesh about six inches. This was still not enough. So with Olivier du Pont remaining nailed to his fallen horse, he struck him other blows as hard, tore the helmet from his head and finally put his knee across his throat so he could not move. Then drawing for the first time the sword that Melusine had given him he raised it over his head.

"Surrender, felon, or I kill you!"

"I would rather die at the hand of a valiant knight than from another," said the young Olivier, exhausted, with blood and sweat running down his face.

Raymondin was moved to pity.

"On peril of your soul, did you know anything of your father's treason?"

"I was not born when all that happened, but despite my ill fortune I still believe my father innocent of the treason of which you have accused him."

Thus he banished the pity that mounted in the heart of his adversary. His anger renewed, Raymondin struck him furiously several times with his gauntlet on his temples to stun him. And when he supposed he could no longer put up the least resistance, took him by the feet and dragged him out of the lists. Approaching the scaffold where the king of the Bretons presided he asked:

"Sire, have I done my duty?"

"By St. George, you have acquitted yourself right marvellously."

And the king ordered they hang Josselin du Pont and his son Olivier without delay.

But the old felon cried piteously for mercy.

"You can perhaps receive grace, if you admit the truth of the quarrel."

"Sire," replied Josselin, "I wish to hide nothing. At this moment the truth chokes me yet forces me to speak. The affair took place as the knight has told. Now, Sire, since I have admitted it, dispose of me but spare the life of Olivier, who was not even born then! It would be for nothing. He is perhaps dying already. Tell me quickly that my life that you take will save that which remains of his."

"There has been much evil on your part, Josselin, and had it not pleased God to let you be chastised as is going to happen, he would not have allowed you to live for so long. You cannot escape just punishment for your double crime. For not only did you provoke the death of the nephew of my predecessor, you calumniated the valiant knight who killed him without intending to, and forced him into exile like a thief, which he was not. A double villainy, a double chastisement. You will be punished twice, once in your own person, another in that of your son, in your body and in your heart."

And he gave the order to hang the two felons without delay.

Raymondin bent his knee before him.

"Sire, thank you as I must for your good justice and the law that you have exercised at my request. But if I may merit anything, I beg you to spare the life of Olivier. Witness his rare valour, worthy of a more just cause. Certain that he has not been soaked in the treason of his father, I cannot bring myself to see him perish, his death would be a great sadness for me. As for his father, he is old and feeble, I forget the felony to see him repent of it. He has no more than a few years to weep over his fault. He has hardly enough white hair to hide his tears. Sire, grant him mercy too! The money that he will restore to me, of his inheritance, fruits and profits, employ to found a priory and pay monks to sing in perpetuity for the rest of the souls of the guilty. Mercy for Olivier! Sire! Mercy for Josselin!"

The king of the Bretons descended in order to raise up him to his feet. When he had done so said:

"This pity gives you even greater credit if that were possible, O knight with a great and generous heart. But I who reign have not the right to accede in this. I cannot do it. I will not do it. Even if I desired it, like yourself. From an evil tree comes evil fruit, and evil within shines beyond. Evil fruit, evil seed, evil grain. And so it goes, and thus be it! No. By the faith that I owe to the soul of my father, never will Josselin or Olivier do more treason to anyone in the world. And to be well sure of that from now on I thus impeach them and leave them to the gibbet. It awaits them and claims them."

And so they were hanged.

Their lands reverted to Raymondin as the inheritance of Henri de Léon, his father. He gave homage to the king, thanked him again for it and for having permitted all. He then asked the right to make a gift of the barony of Léon to his cousin Henri, so that the land would always carry the same name, that of its rightful lord. And while the King agreed, everyone marvelled at Raymondin's natural generosity.

"He must have very great domains and solid means to act in such a way," they said.

Interest grew when they saw his gifts, which included – as he loved them – a great golden cup.

But he was not jubilant, visit and victory were now accomplished and so the lord of Lusignan decided to take leave of the King of Brittany's hospitality.

There were no more direct traitors with which to deal. But the mischievous unite more easily between themselves and Josselin du Pont had formed a gang. Like master, like servants, very often. The chief gone, they continued his work, at least for a time, while they dispersed to find another leader. Although good in itself, wealth becomes indispensable to those who cannot live with themselves and their own empty ugliness. Their constant greed inclines them to crime, and that is just what happened, as the lord of Lusignan discovered on his return from Nantes through the lands of Léon in order to install his cousin Henri there, where at Quéméniguant fine feasts took place to acclaim him, for now Brittany knew him, it was determined to cherish him.

But there is also a good God who watches over the righteous, in His way, not theirs. On the evening of the day when the lord of Lusignan was about to leave, a man came to find the son of Alain de Léon and asked for a secret interview.

He obtained it through his good resolute manner and said: "Four days ago in the forest of Guérande, near a place held by the châtelaine of Arval with two hundred men at arms, I heard one of the valets tell his comrade that, come what may, their leader and his men waited to ambush a certain personage when he passed."

Henri quickly sent a messenger to make sure, who when he returned, warned of the presence of not two but at least six hundred men at arms, hidden at different places, principally along the forest track in Guérande that was traditionally called that of the Crafty Dwarf. He swore him to silence and warned only his brother, so, when the lord of Lusignan left, in the midst of the blessings of all, he placed him, as when he had arrived at Quéméniguant, between his brother and himself, without him knowing anything. He did not know, in particular, that behind his knights, his men and his pages, two hundred men at arms, raised in haste, followed about an hour later.

Warned by his spies, the châtelaine of Arval rejoiced in the depths of his evil heart, and assured his followers that no one would escape and swore to them all to believe that this was true, in view of the proverb. "He who seeks vengeance will achieve it!"

Now the old knight to whom Melusine had committed the safety of her husband came to see him.

"Sire, listen to me. It would be best if you rode armed through this forest, where Josselin's relatives, who do not love you, could perchance bring harm to you all unless you are prepared for immediate defence."

Raymondin protested, dreaming of mercy for the guilty, and not believing this, asked what had led him to think this.

"I do not know how to explain to you, but I know it well, and hold it for sure, thanking God from whom it must come. What do you want, sire! The more I think about it, the more I feel that misfortune will come to us at this place, if we do not take guard."

Many no doubt thought the same; the order was passed to arm and unfurl their pennons in the wind, and Raymondin saw that many were already ready and was greatly surprised at this. Then the two brothers told him what they knew and he was greatly touched, asking them always to remember, in any place or at any time, of the complete aid that he would always offer them.

The conflict took place at three o'clock in the afternoon.

Six hundred men at arms of the evil lord of Arval had concealed themselves on both sides of the road of the Crafty Dwarf, for the whole of its length. His knights' foot soldiers were furious and appalled to find that those whom they had been assured would be surprised were in fact armed. They had thought to rush out, and treacherously cut the ham strings of their horses or disembowel them, and thus to win with little effort, with club or sword in hand. Now it looked likely to end in a hard battle. To summon up their courage they howled in frenzy, as if they needed to convince themselves that they continued to serve the unworthy lord on whose behalf Arval had summoned them.

"To the death! To the death! Death to the cursed one who caused the shame of Josselin du Pont!"

When the trumpets sounded, Raymondin's startled horse reared up between the two sons of Alain de Léon, and carried its master to the fiercest part of the fight, where the furious efforts of his adversaries pressed the most. In the midst of the thick of them, surrounded by his enemies, our hero struck with cuts and blows before and behind, and the good sword of Melusine piled up the dead all round the place where his horse had stopped. Then the châtelaine of Arval, having seen and recognised him, pointed him out with his lance to his three cousins, who swept down upon him.

"We need to kill him," he cried to them. "With him fallen, the others will not stay or last. Then disbanded in flight, we can take them one after the other, and come back for the spoils."

All four, their long lances lowered in parallel, so as to make a small fan, rushed with all the speed of their ugly intent. Two struck at Raymondin's shield while the other two, their lances broken, struck with mace and sword at his helmet. At the same time the two ash wood lances pinned his left arm under the points that stuck through his shield. He parried the one on the right with his sword, avoiding as well as he could the repeated blows of other bladed arms, a footman plunging his knife repeatedly at the stomach of his horse, looking for a way, with the other hand, to force a sword between the joints in his armour, principally under the knees.

It looked like the end of Lusignan if his horse fell, and all four, having withdrawn a little, now returned at speed, while the villain with the knife tried to strike him in the back as reinforcements came from all sides, confident of victory. They began to strike with sure blows but Raymondin pressed his horse so strongly that it rose for a last time to throw itself at the châtelaine of Arvel himself, who, in a moment of triumph raised his head high and uncovered for a second the space between helmet and armour. There, despite the mail coat, Raymondin drove in his sword with so violent a blow, so sure and deep, that Arvel fell backward, voiding his stirrups, his throat pierced with the blade that had gone through to his brain.

At that moment the old knight Alain and his brother arrived, seeking him anxiously, as the whole battle beyond single personal combat established itself. Those who were there ever remembered it. It was bloody, atrocious, without quarter or mercy. The melée so tight that none could employ his armed flail. The rage of Arval's troops so increased that perhaps they might have come out on top in the end, if Henri de Léon had not been inspired to rally his reinforcements, held apart for a while under cover, to throw them at the rear of the enemy at the best moment. He thus saved all.

Disconcerted at the moment they thought they had gained the victory, disappointed a second time, in consternation and exhausted, the men of Arval realised all was lost. They sought to fly, but surrounded on all sides, were quickly overcome and massacred, apart from a very small number who surrendered, among whom were those of the direct lineage of the châtelaine of Arval, put under guard of the old knight.

The next day, after having hanged those who, having given themselves up and given their word as prisoners, had tried to escape, the rest were sent to the King of Brittany. At Nantes these others were hanged as well, the royal anger not even dreaming of pity before their detestable audacity. Alain de Léon was so keen to see them tread their bare foot way to the place of execution that he cried out, as soon as he heard the judgement: "By heaven, I will not eat before death has come to all of them."

As for Raymondin, he rested for five days in the forest around the Crafty Dwarf, that was called from then on the Place of the Ambush, for no one recalled the reason for its original name. Then he told his cousins his ideas for transforming the place for the better:

"Dear good friends, found a priory here named after the Trinity, where eight monks will be maintained to pray for my father's soul and that of the king's nephew, as well as those who were guilty of this mad enterprise. The king will himself decide the place. When all is built, with a fine chapel, endow eight white monks vowed to live under the eye of God."

Then he took leave of them all.

Raymondin of Lusignan returned slowly, in short stages, as he left the kingdom of Brittany and entered Poitou that he loved. He often took to the wide roads made by the Roman legions, of whom there are marvellous tales. For my part I have heard tell more than once, and do not know whether to believe it, since Rome is still there and dedicated to the true God, that these giant roads were made by another race of men, small and stocky as ourselves, who all came from Rome and returned there. And, at Rome, in the centre of a place they call the Forum, at the place of their ancient origin, they built the most beautiful of their thousands of splendid columns – covered with gold and reflecting the rays of the sun.

HERE ENDS THE TALE OF THE BARD OF PENHOEL

·XV·
Return To Lusignan

Over the centuries there was a mixture of Roman, Christian and German elements in all these lands, unified by a Celtic cement, which was succeeded by a great awakening that manifested in architecture. This architectural renovation was universal. The world rose and threw off its old rags – in the words of the monk Gleber – to dress in the white robe of the churches.

Poitou excelled in the new style as if its masters, or those who came there, had absorbed the oriental lessons of Syria, Persia and Ionia. One can see these influences, which remain in part mysterious, before the main gate of St Pierre de Melle, and Raymondin, whom the architect of Lusignan had initiated into certain aspects of his art, gazed along the arches and vaults, and in the spaces between the decorations at the signs of the Zodiac, notably the two Centaurs, the Fishes and the Ram. The decorations were symbols of the four Evangelists; the bull for St. Luke; the halo'd bird, understood to be an eagle, for St. John; the winged angel for St. Matthew; the lion for St. Mark.

At Limalonges, at Champdeniers, at Saint-Pompain and at Frontenday-l'Abattu, he made his devotions, and at St. Hilaire de Melle he admired the arches of the interior, like the capitals of the windows of the lateral façade, and the door on which a painted knight seemed to represent himself, or his companions, under capitals of the arcade, garnished with leaves and ornate interlaced carvings. The archivolt was adorned with lotus leaves in the form of palms, and lower down, among diverse ornaments, were birds that plunged their beaks in the throats of two dogs, and animals that devoured a man.

He was astonished by a beautiful a church at Clussay which he had not noticed before, and saw by its stone that it was very new. When he asked about it the old knight only replied with a smile, and called the men of the village, who told him it was by Melusine, who had built it in a few days. More astonished than he would later be at Lusignan, he pressed a workman persistently with questions, who in the end told the story to him.

"We don't know how sir, but she came one day on horseback and set to work so quickly that the church seemed as if it were growing by itself. Ah, if you could have seen it! She carried the earth and stones she needed in her apron, and so things went until, in less that eight days, it was finished. And once, when she took too much in her apron, it split under the weight and she dropped all it carried. You can see down there on that mound, the pile of stones she dropped..."

And the workman added "Have you really not heard about it sir? Everyone knows about it round here. And in other villages throughout the country are others built with her hands." And Raymondin, after looking long at the masonry arches and the tower that rose above the door, entered and kneeled under the dome.

After St Laon de Thouars and St. Médard, where the porchway is so beautiful under a great rose, after Parthenay and Notre Dame de la Coudre, he stopped at the astonishing church of St. Jouin des Marnes, where the monastery dates from 425 and it seemed to him he had never seen a more impressive nave.

The church of St. Jouin, started by the Benedictine brothers, was a marvel. From its façade, from base to summit of the triangular front, which crowned three arcades and round columns separated by circles, sculptures of fantastic animals arrested the pilgrim. He prayed to their angels, one of whom raised a hand and finger pointing towards the sky, indicating their common origin. And on the same line he gazed upon a beautiful woman below, the fingers of whose hands touched two long tresses of her hair at her breast. So elegant, sweet and perfect that Raymondin, after all he had been told, thought he recognised in her the figure of Melusine.

But above the window was a naked woman with hair falling on her shoulders, seeking to repulse serpents that enlaced it, sucking at her swollen breasts, making her wince in pain, her teeth chattering in despair. Here Raymondin recalled, he did not know why, his apprehensions in the forest, when he was taken with doubts about her, and he also remembered his brother.

But he suppressed the painful anxiety that rose within him before the figure of a woman in a floating robe, standing before a horse ridden by a man whose cloak billowed in the wind. He saw in it the symbol of the wife who awaited him; and in the knight, leaning to one side from the back of the animal that carried him, he recognised himself, urged to return. And it seemed that it was Melusine who spoke to him through these images in stone.

But the stones also represented Religion, in a figure rising above a long line of statuettes, grave and majestic, who carried a globe surmounted by a little cross to express the abundance of Eucharistic grace; at either side, two persons kneeled awaiting the blessing – which gave hope to others advancing to take part in the great initiation. Above, Jesus Christ stood between two angels below him. And in the highest part of the edifice, was a triangle.

Having made his devotions Raymondin left, but continued down the south wall on the outside with its beautiful windows adorned with bands of deep mouldings and, at the end, at the transept, it appeared to him that the work, hardly finished, made this part of the church a fortress.

Before leaving, standing at the foot of the apse, he savoured the magnificent view of the meadows, fields, and woods that he was about to cross with his escort, towards Montcontour, where a keep had begun to be built.

But first the old knight, with the same strange smile as before, urged him to visit St. Pierre of Parthenay le Vieux. Intrigued once more, he questioned him, but received no reply from the knight, who contented himself with accompanying his master before the decorations of leaves and stars, of mounted knights, of chimeras and goats, of animals with great tails, of birds with beaks returned on their backs, and under the leaves, carvings of little beasts whose heads recalled cats or lynxes as well as rats and pigs.

The exterior archivolt carried busts of women with veils, turning their heads a little towards one another, as if they wanted to embrace. There were also tigers, and a man trying to repulse the fantastic beasts and other advancing birds, a Samson aiming to tame a rearing lion, a lord on horseback, falcon on fist.

The church was served by nine monks, who obeyed a prior from the abbey of Chaise Dieu, to whom it had been given. As Raymondin meditated before all these signs an old monk came out, and Raymondin asked him:

"Father, I would like to know the history of this church."

"It was built…"

But the old monk, who had raised his head a little to look at him, paused; for until he began to speak, lost in his prayers, he had not even noticed him. Fixing him with small clear red rimmed eyes, so clear that they made one think of the look of St. Paul, from which it was said nothing could be hidden:

"This nave is a daughter of prayer, of piety, of repentance and of work. Its story, which interests you, would take long to tell, longer still to understand, for a lord who appears to be in a hurry, as you seem to be, at least in the depths of yourself. To know simply what is without doubt the most remarkable, this façade, its vaults and the bell tower was built in three nights by a lady of the name of Melusine. She worked only by the light of the stars, without stopping. One night, surprised in her labours by day break, she left at the gallop on her horse, that in fleeing, left the imprint of its shoe on the stone she was trying to split, which was the last. Here it is. You can touch it with that fine sword that I see hanging against the flank of your horse. Vainly, ever since, the master masons have sought to fill the gap that remained, but any stone put there by them always falls, and its place can never be filled."

It was now evening, and it seemed to Raymondin that the old monk, going on his way after replacing his hood over his eyes, went from him like an uncertain shadow. He followed at a walk on his horse as the old monk approached the cemetery and entered. But Raymondin, who also went in, searched for him in vain. Was it nightfall, that seemed to extend over a tomb of earth where he had prayed? Was it the shadow itself that had been absorbed? He ended by asking himself if the old monk was truly living. But as he thus reflected, it appeared to him that the light suddenly brightened over his head and, looking up, he saw that a light was lit mysteriously, of itself, at the top of the column of the dead.

He rejoined the old knight and his escort, and at last, by long rides and short halts, they arrived at the abbey of Mallieres, where two hundred monks received him with respect, as their child and their lord. Until he, eager to see again she who had watched over him as well as building such curious churches, regained the Fountain of Thirst that had become the Castle of Lusignan.

he tower of the keep, although it dominated all the forest of Colombier, was not obvious from outside, even from a hillock which overlooked the woods, for it had been conceived and constructed to blend in with the highest branches of the trees. Raymondin thus learned, after a long absence, that one can have lived a long time at home and appreciated much, yet without knowing all its advantages. But it was written in the great Book of Fate that his life would be made up of continual surprises, for as he advanced through the forest approaching Lusignan, precisely at the place where he knew there to be the entrance to a tunnel, he now found a fortified village.

He, who had sighed more than once in the course of his journey that so beautiful a country should be so little inhabited, even unpopulated, rejoiced to see that Melusine had realised his desires, as if divining them, and wanting to bring them about. However, all looked so different and new that he began to ask himself if this really was Lusignan and he ended by expressing some of his fears to the old knight, who responded with the same mysterious smile. But as his master persisted, this time he spoke.

"Do not worry sire, you will soon be happy to be there!"

And he saw coming towards them a crowd of knights and squires, elegant ladies and maidens. The knights advanced under the pennants of their colours which fluttered round their lances like little pieces of blue sky. The ladies and maidens under their veils, which floated in the wind, gave the impression of different coloured clouds, and as it was the hour of twilight, each carried a hawk on her fist.

They all cried together: "Welcome, my lord!"

Once more he could only doubt, and once more kept his silence the better to take in just what seemed to be dream and what was reality.

"Beautiful maidens, ladies and fine lords, where do you come from?"

"Sir, we come from Lusignan."

"Is it far from here?"

Then all smiled in the same way as had the old knight.

"Lusignan is before your eyes, my lord! You have not seen what has been accomplished in your absence, but here is someone who can tell you."

And they parted to let Melusine pass through, with her ladies of honour.

She wore a long blue robe, the blue of the sea when the sun is shining but a few clouds darken it a little, as if to deepen our dreams like itself. It was bordered with a narrow white fur, mixed with little white swans' feathers. Her robe opened on a dress embroidered with green and violet flowers, the green in the form of primroses, the violet of campanulas, that revealed the cleavage of her breasts where the corsage opened on a sweet square plunging neckline. The striking fresh oval of her beautiful face was illuminated by her golden hair, under a bonnet of Alençon lace covered with black velvet, from which a plait fell straight on each side and behind her shoulders. And all made angelic by her eyes, on this day more especially the colour of periwinkle.

Her greyhounds surrounded her, and a zebra came before her from time to time, stretching its head as if to be stroked, which made the little hawk fly from her fist, to hover with beating wings above its mistress before returning to its place; while the dogs raised long muzzles, showing their teeth, their eyes fixed on her as if to signify their adoration and submission.

"My lord," she said in a delicate voice which dominated all, "I bid you great welcome along with the rest of your court, who have waited impatiently for you a long time. But no less than I myself, so happy to see you again, to find you present at our feasts and to give you joy. We congratulate you for acting so well and valiantly during your journey, for there is no one here who has not heard tell of your glory."

"My tenderly cherished lady," replied Raymondin, "you alone inspired me in the midst of my adventures, and still more on this fine day when I finally join you again. So let us not speak of me or my merits, for it is only by you and the grace of God that I return safe and sound after all these fights. For which I thank you and God."

At Lusignan, in the fine and strong castle, they lost no time in celebrating their happiness at his return. For eight days they revelled unrestrainedly, and eight more when they made merry more soberly, and finally eight when they returned more to the world and to their affairs. They gave lesser feasts than that of the wedding but more intimate and agreeable, to which were invited the Count of Poitiers, the Count of Forez and the lords round about. Well satisfied to have taken part, all thanked him at length at the hour of their departure.

Then the routine of everyday life took over and continued, regular and serene.

Melusine, with child a second time, produced another boy, named Odon, well formed, apart from one ear being larger than the other.

A year later she had a third, also very handsome, except for one eye placed higher than the other, and he was called Guy.

The fourth – for she only had sons – was called Antoine, and had a birth mark on his cheek in the shape of a lion's paw.

The fifth, Regnault, very remarkable, had but one single eye, but was excellent otherwise.

Geoffroy, the sixth, a rare force, had from his earliest days a great tooth which came at least an inch out of his mouth.

Froismond, whose nose had a small mark, furred like the skin of a mole.

Then after two years rest, Melusine brought to birth an eighth boy who was stranger than all the others; he had three eyes, one in the middle of his forehead. Afterwards he showed himself so cruel that he killed two wet nurses in four years.

During the time that she had these sons, Melusine increased her lands in proportion to their progeniture. It was in anticipation of these acquisitions that she had, during Raymondin's absence, made the various journeys when she had built the churches. Thus the castle and town of Parthenay, the castle of La Rochelle, then yet more towns and fortresses – Saintes, Pons, Talemont, Tallemondois. So many that as far as Brittany and Guyenne and Gascony one would hardly be able to count them all.

As for the children, all were well brought up and encouraged despite their peculiarities, or perhaps because of them. At 18 years old, Urian dreamed only of adventures. He was not so ugly, despite his short wide face, his different coloured eyes, and his enormous ears. He showed ardour and remarkable good will, and he and Guy, the third, were great companions and much adored by the country.

One day they learned that the sultan of Damascus had besieged the king of Cyprus in his town of Famagusta. He was said to be in distress, and although able to resist for a time, was concerned that no one in Christianity sought to help him. The dream of doing so excited them very much, as did the assurance that this excellent prince had for heiress a ravishing young girl.

Raymondin and Melusine gave their consent to the enterprise and in the port of La Rochelle a small fleet was prepared, well provided with vitals, artillery, sailors, and horses, and four thousand men at arms, fifty of whom were crossbowmen – for against infidels the interdiction of the pope against this perfidious weapon that killed at such a distance, did not hold.

All went fast enough. Soon the standards and banners floated in the wind, the trumpets sounded, the horses embarked and they prepared to raise anchor at the first favourable wind.

The fleet was beautiful to see, well composed, diverse, ready to respond to all needs. It consisted of two dromons, two galleys, three chalandes (of which one was a simple chalande, one a challande-pamphile and one a chalande-huissier). Four little gaudes joined the expedition for a time, probably as far as Fontarabie, held close to the galleys and built like them. Finally two great ships, in the form of caravelles, one of two hundred and fifty tons, the other almost three hundred, which dominated the rest. It was truly an admirable navy.

The dromons were, at the same time, war ships with rams. Long, wide in proportion to their height, they carried two ranks of oars, superimposed; they had twenty five seats, measuring almost forty metres long by four and a half wide and weighing about one hundred tons. Of the two in the fleet, one hoisted at the mast a triangular sail attached to a spar at the other point; but both, painted a light yellow, carried proudly at the curve of their prow the figurehead of a tall black sea horse.

The galley recalled the ancient liburn; it had only a single row of oars, but being small, went fast across the water. It proved less rapid however than the simple chalande with its one hundred and fifty sailors, its two ranks of oars, and its extraordinary length, for it was one hundred and fifty feet long, twenty four wide, and fifteen high. Its hundred oars, also long, divided in fifties, each manned by two men, were divided into fifty at a higher stage and fifty at a lower; the lower oars were twenty feet long, the higher ones thirty three. The chalande pamphile carried one hundred and twenty rowers and the chalande huissier one hundred and eight. These three merchant ships, with their stages of oars, were armed at the prow with a formidable ram and at the mast with a little castle for attack and defence. The chalande huissier was wider, more rounded, to take on the horses, which had been embarked by a door situated at the rear above the waterline.

From stem to stern all these fine new ships were painted in lively colours the length of their superstructure, with varied animal figureheads, along with the grey and black ropes of their sheets, stays and rigging. Their sails at foremast, main mast or mizzen in diverse colours of white, amaranthe, red, brown, one of dark red with numerous decorations, ornamented with gold and silver, in the form of seals and coats of arms, or stamped on staysails and girouettes – were like a moving garden on the sea.

It was armed, moreover, and carried to port and starboard all that was needed to kill, notably those varied engines of war that discomfort enemy ships and in sieges used to demolish walls, balistas of great size, protected with mantelets of cord and horsehair. There were also flame throwers for greek fire. Others yet of which one had never heard spoken and which were yet to be tried out. They were charged in their breech to receive a powder which had been sealed in secret and which, on taking fire, expanded with such force that it expelled lumps of iron, or great polished stones, capable of striking down a whole rank of men or weakening a wall by striking holes in it – and no armour could resist it.

On the day of departure Melusine and Raymondin, with their children, stood at the edge of the sea. When all was ready, Melusine embraced her two sons passionately, and gave each of them two rings. One with a sapphire because it conserved the heart, protected against poisons, fevers and wounds and at the same time encouraged joy; the other with a tiger eye, because it attracted riches and maintained them.

"Wear them always," she said. "I have enclosed within them all my love and all my thoughts, that will thus always be with you, and by them you will also keep in touch with me. Wearing them will bring you loyalty, without thought of evil doing or trickery, and you will never suffer discomfort or be defeated. Have always only honourable quarrels. No enchantments, no curses, no person can harm or deny you if you suffer their looks whilst thinking of your mother."

They knelt to receive her blessing.

When they rose she said to them once more: "My children, my dear children, I pray you, wherever you may be, never forget to attend mass before undertaking anything. Prayer comforts, and Heaven protects more willingly those souls who think of it. Also keep to this: help and advise mothers and their works. Honour ladies. Protect orphans and comfort oppressed maidens. Be humble, sweet, courteous toward everyone, above all to the poor.

"Do not neglect to help with thoughtful alms the unfortunate in the grip of poverty, and with intelligent attention and tenderness those who suffer sadness. Embrace the good, pity the unfortunate. When you give, do not take long to do it, for the good ought not to make the unfortunate wait in their need. But forbid yourself, wherever you are, from useless largesse and folly, for heaven has not put riches in your hand to sow them where they do nothing.

"Hold always to your promises in complete loyalty, and enter into them with considered agreement, do not consent to lightness. Do not let yourself be governed by the passions of young men. If you are weak, if you even come to fail, take care that it is not irreparable. Do not covet another's wife, so that one day they do not covet yours. Love those who may hate your foreseen prudence, give freely to those who love you. Hate vice, hypocrisy and cowardice – along with wickedness, the most execrable things in the world.

"Thus my beloved, you will always live honourably. And unless you should perish, which only God knows or wills or permits, you will depart with a heart at ease, conscience clear, almost joyfully. And my children, you will have been my true sons and done your duty. He will otherwise protect you and make you happy."

She held them close for a long time, then added in a whisper:

"There is in this ship of yours enough gold and silver to pay your men well for four years. Good food of all kinds also, special bread, salt meat, sweet water and vinegar. I have foreseen all and am sure I have forgotten nothing... But now we must part!"

Raymondin wept, embracing them in his turn. Melusine stayed where she was, incapable of movement, as he accompanied them as far as the little barque that awaited them, for their parting took place at the end of the last sea wall. When he had seen them on board, he returned to his wife and, leaning one against the other, they looked to sea where the strong caravelle, which had waited till last, the rest of the fleet having already left, carried their sons away.

It appeared on the waves like a rare almost supernatural thing, for at that time no one had ever seen a ship so great as three hundred tons in such a form. It was round, as if cut at the back, but lengthened with a long, high castle as superstructure, with another, even longer, at the fore. Rigged with four masts and a bowsprit, its vertical masts were that of a foresail with square sails, then the main mast, mizzen and counter-mizzen with lateen sails, whilst its three side sails, filled with the wind, obscured the masts themselves and had the appearance of raising the ship towards the sky on the waves of the sea. From the hull to the tackle the ship was painted or embossed with coats of arms, for its wooden hull had been covered with plates of brilliant copper, with golden badges depicting a siren swimming under three stars, and the sun made all shine brilliantly.

On the sea it was like an immense enchanted metal bird with the figurehead of a winged unicorn with head lowered as if to exorcise the waves and dominate them, pointed in line with an enormous long ram of gold plated steel. Large silk banners of all colours floated at the top of masts that were covered with silver leaf. The sails bore at their centre, painted with long purple letters in a gold circle, the device of the two brothers "Faith & Victory" and the purple of the device and that of certain ropes seemed to correspond. In all, the caravelle, as it advanced to rejoin the fleet was like a cradle of hope in the conquest of the East.

·XVII·

The Count of Forez

They lived long happy days together for a long time.
Days that passed so happily that nothing menaced their
tranquillity, like a blue sky ever without cloud, or a clear steady
flowing stream. A sky, so deep in its limitless blue that it would absorb any
possible threat. A stream, so clear despite its depth over a bed of pebbles,
from which no mud was raised, or was ever choked by dead leaves.

Their happiness was such that when day came, whoever arose, smiling,
radiant no doubt, too happy perhaps, without even knowing it, did not
bother to reflect on it. Raymondin knew no more about his happiness
except that he lived it, and nothing of Melusine save that he loved her.
And both felt more and more deeply and irresistibly for each other.

At the same time, he recalled the promise that he must keep, for what
became of a knight who broke his word? At the same time, he realised
that he might not always be constrained by this. And he feared the hour
when he might no more be faithful to his word, or master of himself.

Thus he ever struggled and Melusine, who knew what was going
on beneath his silence, might perhaps have foreseen the time when an
enemy breathed the counsels, or that which had already passed should
be renewed again. For we only control part of our destinies, and alas
cannot foretell all, either for ourselves or for others. Our most subtle
plans are played out against the hopes and fears, the support or betrayals,
of those who love us or who hate us. Even when we think to do well by
approaching someone to pose a question as a warning to him, we may end
up with a result contrary to our intentions. The more so when our words
or our visit come unknowingly or unconsciously from a twilight level of
malice or self-interest, of false sympathy or jealousy, from more or less
repressed feelings. And thus it often happens that our misfortunes come
not only from ourselves, or ourselves alone, but in response to a certain
fact, an external reality rather than something secret within ourselves,
that brings us to decisions against our will, on hearing, accepting and
believing things that are not in our interest. For that which must, will
come to pass one day. One evil day.

Raymondin and Melusine were at Lusignan, back from a visit to
Marmande, on a Saturday at the evening hour, just before the count of

Forez arrived at the castle to visit. This began well enough, for Raymondin had not seen him for a very long time, and his fraternal feeling was strong along with his natural affection and desire for friendship – which brought about a certain forgetfulness of memories that were strong in others and eager to conserve them.

"Where is my sister?" asked the Count, seeing his brother eating alone.

And thus his brother, at the same time as being pleased to see and to stay with them, came out with the key question that raged within him. For there it was before him, like his own jealousy in its worst form.

And as the question was put so directly, it was necessary, whatever he said, for Raymondin to reply. But he seemed to lose his interior strength as he followed the course of his reflections. He began to ask himself how he had been able for so long not only to accept the situation but even to forget about it through his confidence in Melusine. He paused, frozen. Did he no longer possess her? Evidently so, just as much, it seemed.

His wife wanted only his happiness. She only disappeared on a Saturday for honourable reasons, predestined perhaps, but which served his happiness. Predestined? But why? Predestined because their punctual regularity was hardly framed with caprice or for pleasure ... or was it the case of a pact? In which case, what?

Finally, was it necessarily honest? If so, what prevented him from knowing about them? Such an arrangement could come, deceitfully, from the Devil...

No, Melusine, so active, even during his absence building churches, was too good a Christian. And anyway, if there was anything behind it, unimaginable, incomprehensible, their life together would not have lasted so long.

It is true that the Chaplain in this followed old Arbatel, who had left some time ago for the otherworld where he had no more need to pursue his occult researches, since he now knew at first hand what he had been seeking – here Raymondin could not resist a smile in imagining his discussions with the leech Hesnin la Panouze, also now dead, and who had been jealous of him. He had repeated frequently that the Devil possessed all roads, above all the most secret and least apparent ones, and in the end was only ever vanquished in the final place – at one's last extremity.

At this point arose the disturbing vision of his children, that almost tore him apart. Each one had a strange defect, like a mark of Lucifer. He told himself that the type of relentlessness of his wife to build churches so quickly, profiting by his absence, could be interpreted as an expiation and a protection – thus the statue of Religion, the snakes, the fantastic beasts and such sculptures that had impressed him at first, and moved him even more when he realised their origin. His head spun and he almost fainted as he began again almost to persuade himself of the error of his ways. She could not employ her time evilly when she hastened to her religious building and, as for her absence on a Saturday, each time she appeared to regret the moment of her departure and to look forward to her return. And never failing to do so, ever. For each time, at dawn, or in the morning when he awoke, he felt her in their bed, as if she had never left it. In fact, aided by familiarity, he did not even notice her absence.

But still he said nothing, and the Count of Forez repeated his question: "Brother, where is my sister?"

Raymondin asked himself if she was not at this moment occupying herself with charitable works, as he knew her to be merciful. And, all things considered, why part of his being came up against that which he did not need to know, since they had so well and happily lived in their own way. And if betraying the oath could bring disaster, what was the point?

"What is the matter, brother? Fetch Melusine I pray you. I so much want to see her."

The Count of Forez was leaning towards him to the point that he felt his breath and now Raymondin raised his head and met his look directly.

"She is busy today. And because of that cannot see anyone. You will see her tomorrow. Then her smile and her welcome will recompense you. So be content till then and she will give you satisfaction."

"I will wait then," he replied.

But the Count of Forez waited the return of his sister-in-law with a smile so enigmatic as to seem insulting. He had long felt strangely jealous at the immense good fortune of his brother, and to attribute suspect origins to it. By force of such suspicion, it had even become a certainty in his mind, that sat easily with special motives of a more private nature that he felt toward to his brother.

"Yes, I will await you both," he repeated, and laughed insolently.

Raymondin, at the sound of his satisfied voice, recalled the moment at the marriage feast when he had posed the fatal question. He saw him again, the queen in his hand, at the chess board along with his ironic little dissertation. Then, when he had accompanied them both, it had been the turn of Count Bertrand.

But here and now he persisted, in a pressing fashion, with what he had not then dared to say.

"Raymondin, I already love you as a person, and all the more as you are my brother. Please understand that. Because it forces me, however painfully, to enlighten you on something about which you appear to be in the dark. Thinking only of your welfare, I do not want to keep anything from you, but it is time, high time, that I did so. Before I came, I asked here and there (as was my duty, do not forget that), to take account, to reassure myself, of certain public rumours as well as personal opinions, that you were still the happy man of former times. Now, my dear brother, it is said, and repeated everywhere, that every Saturday evening, when you believe her to be innocently occupied and you yourself resting at ease, your wife, your own wife, you understand, is also stretched out at her ease – in the arms of another – in the delights of fornication. You are too blind or bewitched to ask where she goes, on her own at first but then with another, on her Sabbath. But people, whose eyes are not yet obscured with the same sand as yours, see what it going on, and as you can imagine, they laugh at you. Look, whatever my pain or yours, it is no longer possible to keep these things to yourself. They are repeated and sustained, everyone judging you too complacent: 'Let's go in the evening when our lady, every seventh day, regular, works to adorn the head of our good lord and master with a beautiful set of wooden horns.' So, my brother, it is not to your honour to let things rest, but your dishonour."

Raymondin, pale as death, trembled without saying a word. He rose, fixed the Count of Forez with a stare, pushed back the table and ran to his room, where he locked the door to be alone with his rage, his disgust, his jealousy and his desolation.

Also alone, and sure that none saw slowly mount to his face the satisfied laugh that revealed the true meaning of his preceding smile, the Count of Forez dined with good appetite. Then he picked up his sword, called his men and went down to talk to the servants. It is true that evil and the evil doer rejoice those who hear of it.

No one knew anything of Melusine's past. Alas! If they had! One would not have dared, nor could have destroyed the happiness of the other, and the other could have stayed there.

Raymondin, furious and obsessed, did not know where to turn, while Forez waited seeking other stories to support his evil action, the results of which, and the past, we shall learn together, dear reader. We give the translation of it as it was described in one of the numerous grimoires of Arbatel – for he knew all these secrets – that were lost after his death, but have come down to us, without our being able to say just how.

·XVIII·
The Origin of Melusine

THE MANUSCRIPT OF THE ORIGIN OF MELUSINE

There once lived a valiant king in Albany: Elinas, a widower. As he was hunting in the forest, he came across a fair fountain and stream, the sight of which induced such a great thirst in him that he dismounted to drink from its waters. At that moment he was surprised to hear a melodious voice, moving and beautiful, that seemed more like birdsong than that of a human. He stood silent, ravished by the sound of it. Was the voice, so strangely appealing, meant for him? The thought, however faint, caused him to forget his thirst as he approached the most beautiful lady he had ever seen – even though he had known and kissed many. As she had not yet noticed him, he stopped, and the better to delight in her song returned quietly to the fountain, dazzled by the wondrous maiden, both thirst and hunt forgotten. There he stood, touched more than he could have believed possible. And as if in a dream, stilled by such beauty, cradled by a voice which rose like forest leaves up toward the sky, not knowing if he were awake or asleep, or even if he lived on the same plane as the beautiful damsel, King Elinas remained for some time.

His two hounds, who were missing him, had ceased to hunt and came to look for him, and aroused him by licking his hands which hung by his sides, cold, almost lifeless. The good warm tongues of the faithful beasts, panting and dribbling, renewed at least the attention of their master, even if not the life. He shivered, like those who have been lost in thought, and as memory returned, his heart beating faster, he recalled the hunt, realised his thirst and approached nearer the fountain. A little silver bowl hung from a rock above it. He took it and drank from it deeply.

The maiden had now ceased her song.

His thirst quenched, he turned towards her, revealing himself this time, and said:

"Madam or maiden, for I know not which you are, permit an admiring lord to ask. How does a fair lady like you come to be alone in this dangerous forest? And I am astonished that I do not recognise you, for I know all the ladies in this country for at least six leagues around. So pardon my curiosity. And do not think me displeased. Indeed very much to the contrary. It is just that I have never had the chance to speak to one so beautiful. And as I admire you so much I had to say so. So pardon my indiscretion. I ask only for fear of not seeing you again."

"Sir knight," and her voice was as melodious as her song, "you have not been indiscreet and there has been no annoyance to me. I am alone, it is true, but only because it pleases me to be so. To have company only when I wish."

As she spoke a well presented valet came on a high corsair, leading a rich palfrey which astonished Elinas for it was fit for a king, and he thought impossible for a lady other than a queen to own one like it.

The valet bowed respectfully as he brought the horse.

"Good knight, may God keep you!" murmured the unknown lady, preparing to leave.

Elinas leaped forward to hold the bridle and tendered his other hand, happy that she put her foot in it, which was small, arched, smooth in its leather like her hands in her gloves.

"I thank you sir!" she cried, all smiles, once seated in her beautiful embossed and gilded saddle.

And the lovely maiden made off at a long swinging gallop, leaving the king standing, fascinated, all a-dream, lost in meditation, having almost the appearance of death, yet much alive in spirit and thought within.

He was awakened by his huntsmen, who had not been able to find him as quickly as his hounds, and he came back to himself with some displeasure.

"Sire, the course is ready if you wish to hunt the great stag!"

"Certainly," replied the king, trying to take a grip on himself. Then the charm of the beautiful maiden returned to him, and although he tried to dismiss it, he found he could not do so, so pleasant was the vision.

"Go on ahead," he said to the men who had broken his dream, "I will follow later."

Once alone, the king wrenched round the bridle of his mount without care for anything, and altogether bewitched, his spurs in the flanks of the horse, sped off in pursuit of the wonderful maiden. He went so quickly, led entirely by his instincts, abandoning the hunt but still a hunter, that he soon caught up with her. It was in a very thick part of the forest, more shadowy and enchanting than the other, heavy with silence and fragrance. Where she, who had heard him coming, awaited him with serious intent. Perhaps not wishing to appear surprised, she said to her valet:

"Let us wait, I believe the knight has something he wishes to tell us."

The king, already discountenanced, became even more so when she spoke to him:

"King Elinas," she asked, her eyes with their long lashes on his, "are you pursuing me? Have I taken something from you that I do not know about?"

"Lady, you have taken, you have taken…" he repeated, as if lost.

But then took a grip on himself and said, more collectedly:

"No, you have taken nothing…"

"Then pray excuse me if there is nothing else you want to tell me. You can return the way you came."

Emboldened by the imperative language of this sweet maiden who, he felt, challenged and yet encouraged him at the same time, he cried: "There is, truly, something else."

"Then what is it? Speak up!"

"I am trying to tell you."

She laughed, for a woman well knows what a man means when he comes to this point, and waits only to see if he has the courage to say so.

"I seek not only your good grace," said the king gallantly, "but also your love, fair lady."

"You must think little of it unless you ask in good faith and all honour. No man living could attain my love if his intentions were not worthy of us both."

"Such are my intentions, beautiful lady," he cried. "I would rather die than have you think otherwise!"

When she saw him so truly enamoured, she sweetened her tone:

"King Elinas, if you truly wish to take me in holy matrimony, I will obey you as a wife should, but on one condition – that you never seek to see me when I am laying in with child."

He was now so captivated that he would promise anything.

"So be it, by my royal word!"

Thus it was decided.

Then without delay in useless talk as they were so well agreed, he married her, loved her, and they led a loving and quiet life together. And so thought everyone.

All went well, very well. The people of Albany happy to be governed by such a good king and queen. All showed themselves content, except – may leprosy seize his face! – Nathas, son of a previous marriage, for Elinas was a widower. Nathas hated his step-mother, which, as is often the case, brought unhappiness for all, alas!

The queen – I omitted to mention her name – was called Pressine, and he detested her all the more when she gave birth to three daughters, and even more enraged that she delivered them on his birthday!

The first was called Melusine – here we are! – the second Mélior, the third Palestine.

Elinas was not there when they were delivered, but his son Nathas went looking for him and said deceitfully:

"The queen has brought into the world the three most beautiful girls ever seen. Come quickly and see!"

Forgetting the promise he had made, ravished, curious, quite naturally proud of his fatherhood, Elinas ran into the chamber of accouchement when she was bathing the three infants. Full of joy, he embraced her.

"God bless both mother and children!"

Instead of the delight he expected, he heard only reproaches and curses.

"False king! False husband! You have broken your word! And brought great loss and sorrow!"

Then suddenly: "Alas! I see it was your son, the evil Nathas, who brought you here. So much the worse for him, and alas for you! I am avenged by leaving straight away. So much for you! As for *him*..." – and her voice became implacable – "I will be avenged through my sister and companion of the Lost Isle."

But that is another story and I will continue with this one.

No sooner said than done, Pressine took up her three daughters and disappeared, before the King, overwhelmed, could stop her or even sigh or say a word. Nothing!

She went straight to Avalon, to a place called the Lost Isle, where no man had ever entered, and there she raised her three daughters, Melusine, Mélior and Palestine.

Fifteen years passed, during which time she took them each morning without fail to a high mountain called Elmeos, which is to say in the modern tongue, the Mountain of Flowers. From there many lands could be seen on the horizon, including Hibernia. She held her children to her breast, and in tears, cried, pointing there:

"My daughters, that is the country where you were born. There you could and should have lived honourably, respected, happy, raised in wealth and in honour but for the calamitous fault of your father. Now we are condemned to remain sad, poor and lonely until Judgement Day!"

A day came when the oldest, Melusine, spoke up after these complaints and asked:

"Mother, what wrong did our father do to bring about this pitiful end?"

Pressine told them everything. Melusine followed the tale with great attention, and being an inquisitive maiden, learned all she could about the country, the towns and castles of Albany and all that went on there. Then mother and daughters returned to the Isle of Avalon and went their various ways.

Melusine, left alone, the clever and capable one, and not accepting such long and hopeless misfortune, said to her sisters:

"Think of the poverty we have been put to by our royal father and tell me what you think we should do. As for me, I intend to seek vengeance."

Mélior and Palestine thought deeply:

"You are the oldest and know more than us. We will agree to what you decide."

"I am glad you show such loyalty and the love of good daughters toward our mother," said Melusine. "My idea is that we take our father and shut him up forever in the great mountain in Northumberland called Brumbeloys. There let him rot, suffering eternal misery in his turn."

And so the children, not knowing where all this might lead, as young girls will when believing themselves to be wronged, acted quickly, without doubt or trepidation or alternate plan. And the poor king of Albany, who was not even king any more and lived a blameless life, was taken up and carried off to the mountain.

But – glory to the Heavens that know us and to the Great Judge who evaluates our souls – injustice done in anger, even by mistake, always brings accountability. Thus things come about when one does not fully understand the facts.

Their wicked plan achieved, the three maidens, pleased with their triumph, and believing they had acted well, returned to their mother.

"Do not grieve any more, dear Mother," they said, "over the disloyalty our father once showed. He has been well repaid for it. We have taken him and thrown him into prison, in a mountain in Northumberland from which he can never escape until the Day of Judgement. So now he too will spend his life in pain."

They did not expect the reaction that awaited them.

"Why –" cried Pressine indignantly, "did you dare do that, you wicked hard-hearted daughters? When I brought you up I thought that in learning of the misfortune of your father through myself, you would be moved and wish to see us together again! Shame on you! Who gave you the right to act so cruelly towards the one who gave you life? To him I owed the only pleasure I ever knew in the lower world. So now I will punish you as you deserve, for your pride, and evil, ugly, odious deeds! Be sure of that!"

No sooner said than done, alas!

"You, Melusine, the oldest, I will deal with first, as all came about through your ideas. Every Saturday from now, when the sun sets, you will, from the waist down, become a serpent. This will last until you find a husband who has faith enough never to dream of seeing you on that night from Saturday to Sunday. If you should discover such a one, then, and only then, will the curse end! In which case you may live the ordinary course of human life and die as a natural woman – which is truly a great recompense for a faery cannot die! – and after giving birth to a numerous line that will bring honour and glory to you. If, on the other hand, you should marry a graceless, weak, distrustful man who discovers your secret, you will revert to the life of a faery until the Day of Judgement.

Under this threat, lasting the rest of her days, poor Melusine, in repentance, bent her head in fear and trembling.

"To you, Mélior, I give a rich and marvellous castle in Greater Armenia where you will guard a hawk for hundreds of years. Any knight or gentleman of true nobility brave enough to enter your castle and watch over the hawk, without sleeping, for three days and nights before Midsummer's Day may obtain from you any earthly gift. Apart from enjoyment of your body, be it by marriage or otherwise."

Mélior trembled more than her sister had, without even the power to become a true woman, and remaining a virgin for ever. The poor child saw it as a living death. Alas! Even if Melusine became a serpent on the cursed evening of Saturday, on the other days she at least had the chance, if married to a good man, to enjoy his caresses and more in the happiness of a warm bed. Mélior could never give her body or her heart. Would never become a woman. What worse fate could there be?

"You, Palestine, will be shut in the mountain of Guigo, where you will guard like a watch dog your father's treasure, until a day very far ahead when a knight of our lineage will come to win it, and after having delivered you, use it to conquer the Promised Land."

Palestine did not seem too unhappy. In fact was the most certain of the simple experience, even if delayed, of all that is good and true.

But all said nothing of their anguish before their new lives and adventures.

Thus Pressine ordained:

"I have spoken. Now my daughters, go to your fate!"

And the three maidens left, never to see each other again in this mortal world.

HERE ENDS THE MANUSCRIPT OF THE ORIGIN OF MELUSINE

Raymondin knew nothing of this, which is why he intended to be more sure of his destiny.

Alas, because of wanting too much, so as to temper or even control Fate, one may bring about something worse, leading to despair and regret of that which inevitably comes to pass, without explanation. The necessary order for the world to exist is not perhaps that which men want, otherwise it would already be here considering the time they have sought and wanted it, unless their perseverance has failed at the critical moment through the natural perversity of those who undertook it, or those who no longer supported it. Thus the world becomes a game, and as nothing remains honest, a trick. And thus all being false, the game is unpredictable.

But then, who knows, of God or the Devil, which wants all this rectitude? Alone, no doubt, Our Lord Jesus Christ, who sought it for us and to save us. Again who knows all there is and to what it returns?

As, in 1121, visiting a convent in Burgundy, Peter the Venerable, Grand Master of Citeaux, having heard the monks there maintain that they found no part of Scripture clearly say that Christ was God, in his noble prudence, appeared to hear nothing, and wrote to the Prior, Peter of St. John, his brother and his son, that he saw in this discourse a love of study and zeal for knowledge rather than lack or absence of Faith, but that he had better keep such talk to himself.

As for paradise, who knows what it holds?

A trouvère once asked:

Sire, do you know what they do in Paradise?
Do the ladies there dress in rich furs?
Are those who wish to drink well seated?
    Are they served plovers or roast capons?

And Raoul de Houdence, in *The Dream of Hell*, saw Satan invite to his table clerks, abbots and deans, whom he served with flesh of monks, well fattened by laziness, and also roast usurer, nourished by the theft made from the goods of others, both well fricaséed.

Who knows? Who can possibly tell?

·XIX·
Betrayal

In his room Raymondin paced up and down distractedly, such was his regret and his anguish. He gazed at a fine tapestry which showed birds surrounding a page, on the ground and in flight, in an orchard full of flowers in which the colours of wings and petals combined. But while he saw nothing of that, he noted in the frame, filigreed in thin golden wire, a lively faun with open legs, and on its forehead two long horns that seemed to mock him.

So why not seek vengeance? He ended by taking down one of the short swords from a rack on the wall reserved for arms, and passed it under his belt. It was a sort of carving knife and as the wide blade seemed a little thin, he added one of those short "pierce mails", in the form of a well tempered spike, a round dagger in a handle of hard polished redwood. At once he felt sure of the way to deal with whoever had ravished his honour. And whatever the nature of the struggle, when it came to the end, however perfect his armour, he could, if need be, kill him.

This thought calmed him for a moment, to the point of noticing on the writing desk in a corner of the room under a little window of glass bottle ends, a closed parchment bearing his address, with the seal of Urian. He forgot all, broke the wax and read it. Urian and his brother, for they had both signed it, told their parents of their journey and their adventures, which had gone well. They ended not only by greeting their father and mother, but praying their father to take Melusine in his arms and embrace her long and lovingly, which would make them feel less far away, and express all their thoughts for her, and he himself would be present, dreaming of them at the same time. It was as if this recollection of so sweet a past had come at this point to stop him.

They had been successful in all their enterprises. One had become king of Armenia, the other of Cyprus, through their heroism and the aid of the Archbishop of Famagusta and the Great Prior of the Knights of Rhodes. They had undertaken extraordinary battles by land and by sea, and seen lying on the bottom of the sea, at places known only to themselves, ancient columns down there of incredible purity of line. They had increased their fleet, and formed relations and friendships all over the East. They were in alliance, notably, with the descendants of the famous Obeid Allah, the Mahdi, who founded the Fatimid dynasty, and they described not only the palace of the Calif of Errekada, but the Sahel, which had been built under the sign of the constellation of Leo, defying the sea at the cape of Africa, and extending into the water like a hand reaching out at the end of an arm. They spoke of ramparts thirty cubits high, of a port carved out of the rock, of an immense palace with gold windows, decorated with mosaics, which one entered through a dark vault with six doors, of which one, the last, was of solid iron, thirty spans high, weighing 2000 kintars, studded with enormous nails composed of images of leopards, tigers and eagles, and turning on pivots of glass. As they divined the surprise of their parents, they added to the description the text of the Arab historian who described it, by the name of Ibail-Athir. They recommended a unique almagest, of which they gave only the title, which truly interpreted all dreams. Finally they announced their departure for a central African empire where, beyond seven rivers and seven mountains, the elephants which you led there broke down the defences at the threshold of lands full of gold, which had been brought there in pieces by ants as big as cats.

He paused, overcome. A ray of moonlight that passed through the ends of the opaline bottles of the window lit up the long letters full of arabesques, more than those of the West, as if his children, impregnated with the Orient, had taken a little to Islamic writing. And the cool clear light made some of the grains of gold dust glitter warmly in the ink, which, far from here, had dried it, in the kingdom of Cyprus or Armenia.

How could one believe that all this had its beginning in some kind of unknown infamy, without which nothing like this would have been achieved? He saw again his first coming upon the Fountain of Thirst on that fatal night when he had met, known and come to love Melusine. He saw again the stars whose aspects his uncle had gazed upon, and at the same time was struck by the noble face of Count Aimery, so pale, so white, under the stars. Then like a terrible bristling tornado, the immense mass of the black boar, the fatal spear in his hand, his terror, his grief. Then even more terrible, the silence of the forest under the eye of God – who knows all.

But for now he knew nothing. Could not even imagine what was taking place in his soul.

It was as if his reason, blind to all other issues, was confined to a desperate will to know, which ended almost transforming him into another being. The rest was effaced, lost, for, not only he could no longer think of anything else, his reason had became unreason, and unreason his only reason, as if only this reason could exist. Something irresistible and fatal, that even appeared to him as a necessity, welled up from within him. He could no longer understand why he waited. Suddenly frantic, he rose, pulled the bolt, and rushed through to the door that gave on to the bottom of the little tower. Where it led to he did not know, but it was what he needed to know. Up there, where Melusine went to some assignation, unknown to anyone except herself and her accomplice. The little door violently broken down, he began to climb the stair.

He climbed quickly in his eagerness to strike, his heart pumping under his coat of mail as he climbed the narrow winding stair, steeper and steeper, to the very top. There where he had never been before. Neither he, nor anyone, except her – and – who else? He believed there must be someone, but without entirely believing it. He thought he must get there from the other side. Very soon he would know!

Suddenly a terrible idea seized him. Suppose he came from the parapet, out of the high airs? Could it be the Devil…? The painful thought of what he might be undertaking, despite his grief and shame, slightly relieved his jealousy, and even strengthened him. Ah! If that should be the case he would be sure to win, since he fought on the side of God! And above all, to save her! It seemed to him that when he rescued her she would thank him for overcoming the evil. And with the thought of fighting for Melusine to restore her to herself, he felt elated.

But then he mocked himself cruelly for such folly. And then his original oath seemed to rise before him like the next step, which was almost his own height, and which appalled him in the form of an impossible thing of improbable reality. Stopped in his tracks and out of breath, he leaned against the wall. His heart, that he heard all the more because it beat so strongly, seemed ready to stop. What had happened to all the confidence he had put so spontaneously and naturally in his wife?

That they were the same and ever one flesh, each becoming the other to form a single being, to the point of he being everything to her, and she everything to him. And this making themselves one, including their sons, their lands, all the days of their lives, the nights, the hours, the joys and pains, their happy course. At one with the earth, the whole earth with its trees and flowers, its meadows and woods, its sweet and fruitful soil. At one with the sky and its infinite stars, all the heavens, without limit or end, profound, impenetrable, vast, without boundaries or edges. At one with the whole orb that God the Father holds in his hand, surmounted by a little cross bloodied by Jesus to save mankind.

So brusquely had he thrown himself from his room, only to be stopped here, as if paralysed, by he knew not what within himself. That seemed to want to petrify him like the stone all round him at the edge of this so very high step – put here providentially to preserve their happiness, to halt him here in spite of himself, to wait for Melusine.

But this strange step. Had Melusine passed it by leaping it? How had she cleared it, in what way could she have done? And after this step, he saw another rise beyond it, with others evidently to follow. The stairs turned again, always turning, so tightly, so steeply, so imperiously. He wanted to see how, by what steps higher yet, by what real, and above all singular magic, they led to the mysterious terrace, that he had imagined many times from below. That must be under a plume of the trees that fell back on it. Only leaves could be seen above the ivy and red vine that climbed up from below, with thick branches from which came dark points like flames. And the flames of these cypresses appeared like the tines of an enormous comb that, when clouds lowered towards the earth in stormy days or fine, split or divided them. For the first time he asked himself how they had been able to grow so high, and why? At the same time, his brother's brutal words came back to him, driving him to clamber up the step, hauling himself up by his arms. Then, striking his tinder box, he lit a little oil lamp with a long wick.

The last step was also high. Then three long flagstones, hardly marked, led to a sturdy wooden door. Enormous ironwork across its width passed into the wall as if to seal it. So tightly that the stone on each side of the door, like the wood between, could not be opened or raised, or so it seemed.

He sought in vain for a lock. There was none. No place in all the oak and iron for it to be concealed. No doubt about it. His brother had been right. This stunning certainty thrust into his heart like the knife he carried to stab whomever he discovered.

He did not think for a single second about going back. To see, to know, to be sure. All reduced itself to that.

He continued to examine the door over which he moved the little flame of his lamp. Then noticed an almost imperceptible line between two of the thick polished planks of which the door was made. Even though they were mortised into one another to make one seem like all the rest, there was a tiny space visible at the point of joining.

He pulled out his flat knife, and not daring to make any noise, held his breath as he started to slide in the blade and push it slowly, leaning on it with all his strength and weight.

The blade entered a little, so slowly that he almost began to despair. But he forbade himself to think what he would do next, for he could not, he saw, fully part the adjacent boards. But he might make a crack wide enough to see through! He would soon find out something, no matter how!

As he inserted a little more of the thin blade to enlarge the space he had with such difficultly obtained, it snapped with a dry, clear, crystal sound. Furious at the check, anguished by the noise, he listened, frightened. Then almost relieved by the thought that if he had been heard he would soon learn something, and all would be revealed.

But nothing. The heavy silence continued.

He waited a little, then certain he had not been heard, and nothing would happen, drew his pierce-mail with the rough channelled blade, to continue his efforts against the wood, and as he went back to his work, feeling the sweat on his brow and down the length of his body, cold on his skin as it cooled.

What was behind this implacable door? What happened in there? Was it even the true way to Melusine? In the shadow where the flame of the lamp flickered, despairing at the resistance of the wood, he felt as if he was going mad.

However, nothing else came to mind that was possible for him to do in this place where he found himself. His successful progress so far led him to think that he had struggled well, and was even on the threshold of a new destiny, this time certain. This obscure instinct rose from the depths of the being, invaded it and even dominated his will.

The blade entered better, and engaged the length of three angles already. He had raised it, and putting it back he leaned against it with all his might. Then, wedged against it to get more leverage, he felt the wall suddenly give, heavily and slowly behind him. He had only just time to draw the pierce-mail that he carried with him towards the new destiny that seized him. For in his frantic efforts, he had started a device with his back. And as he followed through, he recalled the similar mechanism in the underground tunnels.

He found himself in a room lit by a pale light that defined nothing. All was golden sand underfoot between bare walls, and although he wanted to go back to fetch his lamp, he heard not far away, in a place that he could not yet see, a strange sound of splashing water. Then, as the wall that had snatched him up did not move any more, he forgot the lamp, and fearful of being seen, stretched out face down on the golden sand, waiting for his eyes to become adjusted to the semi-darkness, which already began to become more clear for him.

Soon, he could see almost everything, and thought himself in another world.

The room was quite large, with high bare walls pierced high and low with little niches which shone through interlaced branches of coral. Thousands of shells in unknown forms, thousands and thousands of pebbles in all colours, including great rocks, were reflected irregularly in the thick glass of an immense rough window of uniform colour, its panes joined by fine strips of metal, that appeared like oxidised silver, shining in places. It was like a sheet of water, a sort of plane detached from the sea, then solidified, and through which passed the light of the shining moon outside, veiled, as if supernatural.

On the sand were black globular objects which attracted his attention. He reached out and picked up one that was close to him. It was heavy and round, but irregular, as if spherical clumps of different size had become stuck together. Looking at it closely he recognised it as one of the meteorites that Arbatel said fell from the moon or the stars – the material solidified, he said, from spinning stars – and were worshiped in Carthage under the name of abbadirs. As he held it in his hand, the sound of water came more strongly, very near. He kept still, to judge from which side it came.

Through a wall of glass behind him a form moved and appeared to lengthen. He noticed that the wall of glass opened at the centre in an arc, a little like the entrance to St. Pierre de Melle, between two high columns which jutted out of it, of bronze or black marble. He slid slowly forward toward one of them, over the golden sand with the scattered meteorites enclosed in their own night. And in the moonlight that made his coat of mail glisten, he had the appearance of a strange serpent with iron scales.

Transported beyond himself, his brother's words already far away, frozen in a cold sweat, hardly alive, and yet held withal at the peak of his very being, sure of knowing from now on. The memory of his oath and of all his preceding life forgotten, he slid, fascinated, toward the unknown source of his misfortune and loss. Eventually he reached the right hand column and, more slowly still, raised his head as far as his eyes above the low wall ran the length of the window on each side of it.

But hardly had he seen than he closed his eyes again, retreating so as not to be seen himself, and in an impossible light, to dream of what he had never seen before, ever. A vision that he carried within him eternally until the end of his days.

So it was he alone who was culpable! It had come to that! He was sure of her now, but too late! The sweat that had cooled him now seemed to descend to his heart and to make it stop.

But before he died, he wanted to see it again. And as all was lost, he looked long, or believed he did, for a minute that seemed like an eternity, to the point of preparing, even colder than himself, his coffin and gravestone. And before having seen all he wanted to see, he noted in mosaic flagstones before him, a great meteorite that, caressed by the rays of moonlight, seemed to take on a form of secret, interior existence. It shone sweetly, polished like a mysterious otherworld fruit. But then the fruit disappeared, as if it had ever been only a dream.

In a long and wide pool set within the dark blue mosaic, decorated here and there with the green leaves of violet and black irises, was the flawless figure of a woman, forever young, whom he knew well. Her bent back magnificent in profile, her breasts raised, as she combed her long golden hair, and the exquisite flesh, more pale than usual, pearled almost to transparency. In her other hand she held a mirror, its crystal reflecting the moonlight on her face, which despite the life that animated it as she smiled to herself, gave it an almost lifeless quality. As she turned slowly, a tail of green scales stretched under the water made the water lilies move, and one of the points came out, streaming with water, like that of a fish.

All around the wall above, the pale purple of Virginia creeper cast shadows on the mosaic and over the water, against the clematis that fell back from all the walls, shining white among the green leaves with clusters of honeysuckle. And thick fine cypress, immobile except almost at the end of its fine points, climbed toward the starry sky. A natural cupola that seemed to break into the mysterious beauty of this extra-terrestrial place, where a subtle perfume floated in the air, unknown but impregnated with the Orient. And it was toward the sky now that Melusine, her mirror dropped into the dark water, that palpitated with the reflections of the stars, stretched up incomparable arms that shone like liquid gold.

He drew back, stretched behind the dark column, his face fallen into the fine sand, which penetrated his nostrils, his open mouth, and grated between his teeth like damp ashes.

·XX·

Forgiveness

How he returned to his room, to his bed, the section of wall returned to its place, the lamp taken, extinguished, flung wildly into the void to fall in the deepest part of the moat, he alone knew, if he even remembered!

Thus this fantastic being he had seen on the terrace was at the same time his wife. Never had he loved her so much in his despair at knowing all was lost, aggravated by his distraught passion at seeing her again so strangely young. Thus never, never had she ceased to be everything to him, and nothing that separated her from him on these Saturday nights was down to her. Thus she was a woman – his own – and she was a siren – also his own – and all that he had here, of the best and the worst in feminine flesh, had never ceased to be his lot. Comprising the most unheard of good fortune that any man had known, made up of the deepest sensual pleasure and the highest most certain virtue. But now he himself had broken it, exposed it, destroyed it! No-one in the world had been so adorable as she and he had shattered her destiny. Nothing was more certain than the future in which he had, in advance, erased all hope for her.

His teeth chattered as he lay in his bed where he could find neither warmth nor comfort and pretended to be asleep as he heard the step that he awaited in spite of all. But he found himself revived as he felt her glide, sleek and warm, next to him under the sheets.

Melusine!

He forgot all his fatigue, inflamed with a desire to turn and hold her in his arms, and avow to her, in ecstasy, the immense joy of never being separated from her or alone, even if this could no longer be. Yet as he could neither speak, nor sleep, he silently muttered to himself the grief that consumed his heart.

"Melusine! You that I love so much, and more, even more. You of whom all the world speaks well, and honours. You whom everyone loves who approaches you and all the more when they see you again! Have I lost you for ever?

"But no, no, since you are here. That accord we have known in our lives together, in ourselves and in our children. The faith we have had in each other, without reserve, has been our strength and cannot die. You are the source of my joy and source of my life, and more than both together. You are the quietness of my days, the happiness of my nights, the peace of my being, the beating of my heart, the wings of my soul, and more than that. You are all, and more than that also and more even yet. Have I now lost all? All, beauty, goodness, pleasure, comfort, understanding and perfect amity, my well being, my hope, my courage, my destiny! All that came from you, my love!

"False, lame and blind Fortune, bitter, hard, cruel Fortune! With a single blow you have flung me from the top of your wheel to the lowest – the place of misery and grief – and all through my fault! I should curse myself but it is you that I curse! You who gave me the most beautiful of beauties, the wisest of the wise, the best of the best, and now take it back from me! Infernal Fortune, sad Fortune, implacable Fortune, enemy Fortune of all worldly blossoming, of all human abandon! How demented whoever binds himself to your service! Who follows you, through a long madness, wholly committed, believing you faithful, counting on your promises, encouraged by your caresses, resting on your bed! Fool and imbecile! You deceive, you betray, you mislead, you crush, you wither! O Treacherous one! There is in you neither certainty, nor stability, no more than exists in a wind vane fixed to the top of a house, humble servant of the least breeze that blows. Alas! Alas! Melusine! Melusine! Melusine! I have dishonoured you, you, my adorable companion, you my greatness and my sweetness, by my treason, for it is I who, suspecting you in this regard, I, even I, who have betrayed you, betrayed and lost. What remains for me to do? … Melusine!"

Thus he silently lamented and as he trembled from it, she leaned across him, and asked:

"What is wrong my love? You are shivering. Have you had a nightmare that makes you mutter so strangely?"

But his teeth chattered all the more, cold, his eyes half open, pale and jaundiced in the grey dawn light that entered the room, that felt to him like an unhappy phantom, imprecise or held back, like approaching Death, ready to carry someone off.

"What is it then? It is me, Melusine! I beg you, what is it? Are you ill? Have you been? Are you now? Say something! Tell me!"

He rallied at these welcome tones, at her concerned words. It seemed to him that hope had suddenly returned. With the same sudden violence as he had felt in his room, and the length of the fatal staircase and into the marine room, that remained in his memory like an enchanted grotto. He realised that perhaps she had not seen him! And knew nothing! He felt life return to him, and come back completely when he had taken her in his arms and anxiously asked her what he might have said. He remembered only a sort of anguish, a nightmare he could not remember.

She pulled herself together too, and with a little sad smile and a voice a little distant, abandoned herself to him in complete tenderness, her body offered at the summit of their rapture:

"My dear love! Keep me with you always!"

And holding on more to the sweetness, and all his, languidly and almost fainting, she murmured, so low that he heard nothing through his elation:

"Ah! If I could only die now!"

For she knew all, having seen first the shadow that revealed him, then his face, frightful, reflected in her mirror. And also through herself, who could not fail to know all, but was shown, after that Saturday on the terrace, to try to deceive herself about what she knew must come.

Thus, for the first time, at the moment even that they appeared the better to understand and know more of each other, and that he knew almost all about her, they were not ready to be more truthful but even to lie to themselves. It needs only one reticence for it to be so, and no doubt, could be more.

And he lied more, for one has only to begin an untruth to become its prisoner.

"Don't worry at all. I perhaps had a little fever while you were away. I don't know why, but I now feel much better. Your being here cures me, Melusine, it cures everything."

She thanked him for his comfort and his courtesy, then, after having embraced him again, she slept. But he could find no sleep and followed again the course of his interior monologue that he rehearsed to himself silently, without even knowing quite what he blamed himself for.

"Poor adored serpent! Sweet unhappy siren! If I was not so sure of having seen you, I would think I had been dreaming. Melusine never appeared to be more a woman than she suddenly did in those moments. Never had she felt so much mine! Never, certainly, so dear."

And he repeated this endlessly, like a return to the mysterious terrace.

When she awoke, later, the sun full in the room, it seemed to him that she looked paler than usual, as if her blood ran thinly, or no more. And when she spoke to him again, he noticed even that her voice, melancholy in its musical diminishing, sounded more distant.

Then he also began to lie to himself.

"Everyone has their days and so was it not quite natural, inevitable, that Melusine was tired? She will appear better tomorrow, after a night's sleep."

The more he reassured himself the more he convinced himself of his ignorance of all that had happened. Everything was now in the past and within a week all would be forgotten! Just as if it had never been! He almost believed this, repeating it every minute, and ended up supposing it to be certain.

Once dressed and ready, he descended from their room full of confidence.

Passing the first drawbridge he met his brother, who was walking with slow steps along the wide stones at the edge of the moat, throwing in little pebbles to see what came up to the surface of the water – moon fish, cat fish, lively little sticklebacks, a few frogs, that appeared and disappeared quickly, and old carps, heavy, slow, almost oily, some which had in their arched mouth a golden ring of water that lit up their greeny greyness.

He appeared concerned, and turned on hearing Raymondin approach, saying quickly, as if caught in the act of doing something wrong:

"I have been waiting… what happened?"

But Raymondin simply glared at him fiercely, saying nothing. He had only to turn a little to the right to be at the foot of the high terrace where everything had recently happened, and his rage was such as to return suddenly – as always – on the author of all these evils, of which he thought no more, but saw appearing all round him. Even Melusine's high keep, that appeared to be tottering and about to fall upon the Count of Forez and crush him.

At first his brother could only repeat:

"And then?"

Raymondin looked him hard in the eye, wordlessly. He had only to push him, a single little shove, and all would be ended, everything. The still water was deep and under his armour he would go straight to the bottom.

"What has happened to make you so pale? … You have seen something you did not wish to … wasn't I right? … Ah tell me, my poor brother I beg you … Tell me what you saw … whatever it is! You need to speak! Just tell me!"

And Raymondin dreamed that he had asked him, even he, to speak in a different way of Melusine. That he too knew all about her.

His face became so hard that the Count of Forez recoiled and looked quickly behind him to see if he still had a place to fly. He continued to retreat round the moat, and found himself under the same terrace when Raymondin started to speak. Just indeed as he had wished, but in a voice of such malevolence as he had never heard, and would not think possible to come from his brother's mouth.

"Go! Leave this place! Fly quickly and never come back! False relative, disloyal brother! You have made me commit an almost irreparable crime. It is, at any rate, for me who, very far from resembling you, belong to the race of those who do not know how to lie, because even when we do, cannot do it well, nor truly, nor to satisfy ourselves. Your duplicitous suggestions, imbecile, grievous, were seeds of punishment from Hell, and extensive, properly understood. For they, through your jealous wickedness, raised my suspicions, even more stupid and criminal than your own, to perjure the most loyal, do you hear, the most pure woman that ever was. Fly! Fly from this place and stay there! Fly where you want, but far, far from here, for wherever I may be I could not even see you without hating you. Save yourself like a thief, for you have stolen my peace of soul and perhaps even my soul itself. Take good care and listen to me, I beg you, as I tell you to depart and leave this house to which you have brought Grief and Evil. Leave quickly all that surrounds you here, for if I did not restrain myself, I would kill you. I will not do it. But be sure you deserve it a hundred times over. Get out of my sight and out of my life!"

His tone was such that after trying to smile, the Count of Forez, paler even than Raymondin, left without even daring to speak or to offer his hand. He retreated at first by stepping backwards, then turned his back, and bent double, ran alongside the foot of Melusine's high Saturday night terrace that overshadowed them both, and so departed.

Now, as it was Sunday, the bells of the last mass, those of his and Melusine's, and those of all the castle, began to ring. But they too had the air of sounding less well, more weakly, as if they were further away from him the nearer he approached them. And at the lordly seat, from where they dominated all, for it was above the bottom end of the chapel, behind a beautiful balustrade of carved wood, it appeared to them, for the first time, that they were far from the altar. But they did not dare look at each other so as to not have to share this thought, or that they did not confess all, neither he to her, nor she to him. And the knights, ladies and maidens found, also for the first time, that beyond their sadness, the faces of their Lords were afflicted with a certain weariness and pallor.

The usual great Sunday dinner in the midst of all the gentlemen, their wives and their children was also marked with a strange discomfort that no one could define. However all stayed and ate well, Melusine like Raymondin. After the meal, she embraced her sons, who went to play at the archery butts, then prepared a hawk for a hunt to be held the following Thursday, so meticulously that some became anxious and asked her if she was leaving on a journey.

To them she replied yes, but they would see her again before long.

And, when alone with Raymondin, she embraced him longer than she had her children. Then she took her leave to go to Niort, as had been agreed, she assured them, even if they did not remember it. And she called there many workers to build that fortress with the twin towers, so beautiful, simple, strong and bare that is still admired to this day. For if it was Henry II of England, or more probably his son Richard, who began the fortress, it was Melusine who joined the two keeps and achieved the perfection that raises it above all other fiefs in the area, of Latour and Mothe-de-Méré, including Fontaine-Epinette, Crémault, Barbeziere, not to mention St-Maxire, St-Pezenne, Souché, Prahecq, St. Hilaire la Palud, Charriere, Benet, Moutiers sur le Loy, Brulain, Aiffres, Echiré, Chef-Boutonne and many others.

XXI

The Younger Sons

Now it happened that Froismond, the younger brother of Geoffroy Great-Tooth, became a monk in one of the little novitiates of the abbey of Mallieres. This put Geoffroy into a great rage when he heard about it. At first he blamed his parents for neglecting their responsibilities. But fortunately – or unfortunately? – his anger was directed against the abbey itself and those whom it contained.

"By Mahomet," he cried, beside himself before the messengers who brought the news, "my father, the Lord of Lusignan and my mother, Châtelaine of the same place, have enough put by to make my brother Froismond rich and marry him off well! God's teeth, those flattering and deceitful monks have bewitched him with their sanctimonious 'let us prays' and 'our fathers', and now, like a rat in a hole, he will never come out alive from their snares or dirty traps, but only stiff and feet first in a coffin, to be buried in their special earth consecrated with monks' piss and holy water. By the Devil," – for he swore unceasingly – "nothing has irked me more than this. I will so pay out these monks for their monkey business that they will never want to make monks again. If it please God – for will he protect them in view of what has happened? – I will destroy the seed so there can be no more re-growth. As for me, I have never liked these despicable and diabolic vermin, who do nothing but fatten themselves on the backs of others."

Thereupon, leaving the tower of Montjoy with his father's messengers and chosen men at arms, he galloped furiously towards the novitiate of Mallieres, which was a beautiful abbey in the forest surrounded by a wall. The high fortified entrance door carried the escutcheon of the religious Trinitarians, which was of silver with a cross alaisée, of which the traverse was blue and the mounting of red on a blue border charged with eight golden lily flowers.

When they arrived, the portcullis of the door was raised, for none thought evil of anyone who came from Lusignan – the brother porter least of all. Thus all passed through.

The abbot and his monks were meeting in the Chapterhouse, gathered round a great beautiful wooden lectern on which the usual eagle, hieratic and fine, carried the Book of Books between its wings, with the monogram of Our Lord as it had first been inscribed in the Catacombs. This in no way moved Geoffroy Great-Tooth who charged fiercely into the midst of the seated company and began to insult them.

"Ribald and deceitful monks, who gave you the right to bewitch my brother Froismond with weasel words to make him a monk in your monkery in your vile image?"

And as, appalled, they said nothing, he went on:

"By the suffering of Gehenna, what you have done, contrary to your calculations, is a bad affair for which you will drink from a bitter cup. And I will see you do – I promise you that!"

The abbot defended himself by swearing in the name of all the saints that Froismond had come of his own free will, called only by the Holy Spirit, which blew where it listed and asked permission of no-one, as was right, since it was in the service of God. And Froismond came himself in his brown robe to attest to his faith, taking an oath on the great figure of the crucified Christ on the long wooden cross, that extended between floor and ceiling at the end of the hall.

To pacify his brother more, he added:

"Never, within here, has anybody counselled me to do so, dear Geoffroy. If you want to take it out on someone, that can be only me, myself alone, and no other apart from God. That is the whole truth, that I confess to convince you. Can you not see? My devotion and will are very simple. It is all so natural when it seizes you one day, you know neither how nor why, and opposite to the ways of the world, when all is said and done. And all this, since you are so incredulous in your wrath, I swear before you again."

His infuriated brother, in the toils of Hell, became only more infuriated.

"By the Devil's hoof then, you will pay like the others. I will not be mocked for having a brother who is a monk, monking, monkery, monkeying, mockery, prating his 'let us prays' like all the idle who lead such fat and useless lives."

"What will you do then?"

"Kill you all, in the Devil's name!"

"Then we will go to heaven," came the gentle response from his brother Froismond, letting his arms fall, then raising his hands, as if waiting martyrdom.

And the other monks and the abbot appeared as resolute, as well as tranquil and blessed, as each made the sign of the cross. Then the old abbot, as debilitated and puny as he was, rose up; and standing upright, raised his plain wooden cross, white and polished, on which he had with his knife, in the way of shepherds on their crooks, marked crosses and stars, and said aloud and simply, in a firm clear voice:

"One brother for another. If Froismond is here, perhaps God has claimed him in order to redeem you."

And added:

"Let us pray, my brothers, so as to understand this mystery."

Geoffroy Great-Tooth broke into a sacrilegious burst of laughter even though baptised a Christian, and left, slamming the door behind him, and with the key that he had taken from the inside locked it with a triple turn. Then he called his men and ordered them to find straw fagots quickly and pile them high under the long, ogive windows. With the feelings of a terrier toward a fox, having decided to grill all, Froismond included, without further process.

The messengers from Lusignan, six knights, interceded in favour of Froismond, when saving the rest appeared impossible. For even supposing the others were guilty of deserving such rigour no blame attached to him. But all to no end, other than render the cruel brother more resolute than ever.

"By the Pope's navel and his old mule, stinking with the sweat of his feet," he thundered, "when all is done, neither he, nor any of them, inside or outside, will sing any more lauds or matins. They will have no need to wake themselves up!"

And once more with a brutal laugh he cried: "On that I am resolved!"

The knights left, so that none could be accused of having aided him in this sacrilege.

When they had gone, Geoffroy Great-Tooth grabbed the little lamp that burnt at the saint's feet in the niche of St Roch, over the door between three great shells carved in the stone. Then, with remorseless hand, put it to the straw.

The flames spread quickly all round the pretty little abbey, made the fagots crackle, and little by little began to climb all around it. And as the monster had taken care to pile most of the fagots against the door, it was impossible for any to escape. The windows, already licked by the fire, began to break, as the lead that bound them melted. And soon, long flames began to enter the building attracted by the dry wood, including the wood of the great cross of Christ.

They climbed the framework of the little bell tower, and detached the great bronze bell, which fell right on the old abbot, sending him without further suffering to paradise, in the midst of the cries of horror of the brothers destined to a harder end, like the greatest tortures of the damned.

They waited with courage, that showed how superior they were to the insults that had been flung at them. All on their knees about the body of their spiritual father, whom they knew must already be praying for them at the foot of the Heavenly Throne. In prayer themselves, they began heroically to chant their own requiem mass, singing the responses one to another. Thus they remained, afflicted by the heat and half suffocated by the smoke, but hardly a single one still singing as the flames began to seize them.

Anyone would have been touched to the depths of pity for these poor monks by the sound of their funeral canticles. But Geoffroy Great-Tooth continued only with his terrible laughter, and laughed more loudly when, after a first silence, the monks on the point of death, and victims of the most atrocious pain, could not repress their frightful screams.

Thus all ended there, by an act of the Devil.

What is more, persuaded, no doubt, by sense of a work well done, he rejoiced at the monks being roasted alive as the smell of human fat began to drift across the suffocating heat of the fire. It did not bother him, not realising that it only proved that he was a minion of hell. Finally the heartrending cries ceased and the fire was master of all, as the walls tottered and cracked and began in different places to collapse. The smell of a mass grave became more atrocious when the flames, at last, diminished, and Geoffroy departed content.

But the further he distanced himself from the fire, which was certainly one of hell and no longer warmed him, he no longer felt quite the same, and began to feel anxious. The conscience that he had lost returned to him, little by little, and remorse grew, at first miniscule, smaller than German elves on nocturnal lakes in the lands of Souabia, or Korrigans along the Rhine, but so pushed Great-Tooth that when he rejoined the knights, whose remembrance and attitude reminded him increasingly of his sin, he could not restrain his sobs. He broke down with the same violence as he had earlier raged – nothing was held in moderation with him – so after being moved to pity, he rose to frenzy, and would have impaled himself on his sword had not his gentlemen restrained him.

"By hell, I am done for!" he cried. "The Devil has possessed me!"

When Raymondin learned the news, and was informed in detail of all that had passed, his first reaction was to disbelieve it. While this impression lasted he had his horse saddled and quicker than the murderer had come from Montjoye, made for the novitiate at Mallieres. Before the still smoking heap of rubble, and the hidden fire that threatened to gain the wall which supported the central nave, he dropped to his knees, appalled. And in doing so, the memory returned of the tragic night when he had fallen his length on the sand that had grated and crunched in his teeth. And he finished by doing the same here, in the grey dust, burning and black, praying God to pardon his child and keep from him all that Fate might have in store.

He tormented himself yet more in the belief that there was no longer anything he could do, as if certain now that everything always finishes badly, always, in this lower world. He returned to his most painful anxieties. He put to himself, more insistently than ever, those shadowy questions. All hope abandoned.

Melusine herself was no longer seen as the harmonious and nocturnal siren of the magic basin but transformed into an atrocious serpent; a sort of infernal sphinx, born with membranous and hairy wings. He began to tremble in all his limbs, without being able to move, nor to rise, his body worn out like himself, weak and lost. For the first time in his life he felt rise within him toward her a new sentiment, that could never before have been born. That would never, until now, have found a place. To make her almost a figure of hate. For he no longer doubted that Love could mislead – or be lost.

And in the grey dust with black stains, the bits of charred wood and burnt planks around him, one would have said that he mirrored on the ground (except that he was still dressed), the great figure of Christ between the walls of the novitiate of the abbey of Mallieres when it had existed when people prayed there. For none now, apart from him, prayed there any longer for the sins of the world and the unhappiness of men. Nor did he dream as yet of any beyond his own.

Rising and remounting his horse, he groaned:

"Geoffroy, my son, my son, what have you done? You had the best beginning of knighthood that could be. Your prowess brought you fame everywhere, of which one only, your killing the giant Guédon, was sufficient to represent your merit. And now, suddenly – forever – you change – and turn from the loyal right way to enter the way of sacrilege! There must be something incomprehensible here. Something not yet known. For how else continue to deceive me? This last blow has beaten me. Plunged now, in every way, in darkness, I am lost in shadows from which I can no longer escape with my reason."

And he sighed again.

"What phantom is she then, this woman who was once mine, who still is, whom I cannot stop loving but who has given me such strange children, all marked with a fatal seal? The last born, today just eight years old, killed two of his nurses by biting their breasts. This one has three eyes; that one enormous ears. Another with hairy patches like a beast…

I know not what! And she, whom I surprised one Saturday, with the bust of woman and tail of serpent. Ah, siren, siren! Was I dreaming? Are they the same, my children? Is this my wife? Is she my wife? Have I not been abused? What is real? What is unreal? What ever is the real? Is it I that exist, after all? I feel myself, and I know no more. I am a son of human nature, I at least. I am come from the womb of a woman. However, all that happens to me is so strange, ever in the domain of the impossible, of the unknown...

Thus he arrived, hardly recognizable, at Marmande, in so strange a state that people sent to warn Melusine.

If they had asked him, what is more, he would have told them that on entering his little castle, built in the beginning for him and Melusine, he had seen on the escutcheon of the arms of his house the different parties who constituted it, who jostled one against another, then disappeared.

Now, all met again. There they were, forming the shield:
1: of silver with a golden cross, cantoned in four croisettes of the same, which is of Jerusalem; 2: barred silver and blue in ten pieces, which is of Lusignan; 3: of silver with a red lion crowned with gold, which is of Cyprus; 4: of gold with a red lion, crowned the same, which is of Armenia.

XXII

Departure

Like them, she was appalled when she saw him, and became so pale she seemed near death. She realised that his happiness was finished, that his heart was broken, that he who had been Raymondin had ceased to exist.

She had returned with all speed seeking to remedy an unfortunate incident and to draw near once more to the one who was her reason for being and her future. But then saw her husband lying there glaring at her with a look of hatred. Although through the open window the scent of an orchard in flower and the fragrance of roses gave her renewed strength, she understood all immediately.

While she spoke he looked at her with eyes that turn and turn about were haggard and staring, or furious and sorrowful, or at times almost tender but quickly replaced with another evil look.

"My Lord, do not despise me! I have never ceased to be and I remain your wife. Do not torment me with this strange silence! Come back to yourself. This is madness, as you know well, and only brings thoughts that destroy you. As for Geoffroy, it is folly on your part, to persist in this distress, you who are rightly held to be the wisest prince living. I feel it myself, but something once done cannot be changed. We cannot go back to it. What is done is done and nothing in the world can undo it."

He still said nothing, but thought apart to himself: "And so she accepts, just like a woman, that which is but should never be! … Ah Siren! … or woman? What does it matter? Women do not know, know nothing of what we call Honour!"

"Yes," she replied, as if she did not notice his disagreement, "that which is done is no more. If Geoffroy, your son, our child, has committed this outrage, it is perhaps not his fault, but of his great courage misdirected, which nothing can stop from the moment that he has made a decision, be it bad … Listen to me! Understand me! Believe me! He has only sinned through too much zeal, for the service and glory of your line, by too much obedience to his nature, which comes from you. He has too much spirit, and very fine spirit. As for you, you cannot blame him.

"He could not see without wrath one of his brothers, whom he loved, cast, abused, ignorant, too good and too naïve, too pious for his age, for even piety has its times and seasons, its opportunities and its days. To see him in the midst of debauched monks, or that he truly believed to be so. And which he dreaded would be a bad example of an evil life, unworthy of us all in every way.

"On the other hand, you have, thank God – and with God's help – all that is needed, and more, to rebuild the novitiate that he destroyed. To enhance it, to renew it with perfect monks, better still than those whom he so cruelly condemned. Perhaps even for their own good – for who knows what is the will of God?

"Geoffroy will amend himself before God and men. He will make them forget through his wisdom in his riper years. That is how things happen with anyone, the excessive fits of anger, immoderate, in youth… My good sweet friend, let go the sorrow that consumes you, and return to the sentiments more fitting to your princely estate, which is to be a shepherd of men."

These consoling words unleashed from him a reaction far from Melusine's expectation.

"False serpent," he whispered, avowing and breaking out with all that she could even pretend, from now on, not to know, or to doubt.

"Yes, serpent, serpent always," he repeated, with outraged harshness, "you are only a phantom, and so is your fruit! None of those who have come from your cursed womb know how to come to a good end, because of the sign of reprobation with which you have marked them by your sins. The only one justly issued from a good angel was poor Froismond, who could bring you pardon for the others. Now he has been burned alive, by his own brother, under I know not what diabolic inspiration. By another of your own sons, I tell you. This terrible and cruel Geoffroy who also carries the sign of his damnation on his face, with a tooth like a fang. And you seek what cannot be conceived, can never be understood, to forget the other to excuse him! Impossible to believe that Hell does not mix the good with the bad, and beyond, into our affairs. And that is how it would appear, you have dragged me down in your fall and I am lost."

Melusine, by this time, found the cup too heavy, its contents too bitter. She could listen to no more. There is no language that has not its limits, more or less agreed, but he had gone beyond them. Carried past himself, and with all else, he could only believe that, as well as from Geoffroy, all evil came from her. The cruel and unjust reproaches achieved that which she had so persistently and sweetly refused to accept, but that had now been unleashed by the perjury of her husband. Decidedly, he had broken everything, destroyed all. Yes, all was finished between them.

And as she could not accept it, the fate that was now imposed on her, she felt everything uncertain, herself, the future, as if her heart was breaking, and she fell to the ground as if she were dead.

He called, and people ran from everywhere.

Frightened at the sight, in tears, for all adored her, they fussed about, and the leech who had replaced Hesnin la Panouze, but whose name has not come down to us, sprinkled her with a special water that appeared to revive her. Very soon he gave her to drink, almost by force, a beverage of cold water in which he had mixed an elixir of herbs culled according to a rite known to him alone.

She came back to herself.

To complain, as her first words, that they should have let her die. And all were yet more saddened, for they felt that she avowed her own true thoughts. She insisted, what is more, on refusing to find in the act that had recalled her to life any charity. True charity, she murmured, would have been to abandon her to her fate, since all reality extended and weighed heavier on her now, more distressing than a nightmare.

"Ah, Raymondin," she sighed finally looking at him, her eyes full of tears, her beautiful face lamentably drawn, deformed, swollen by grief, "the day I first saw you was a sad one for me! Deceived, as women are and always will be, by your handsome body, your honest face, your sweet appearance, I did not suppose you capable of treason, however slight. Now you have foresworn me, you have broken the solemn promise you made.

"However, this treason, this lack of faith, I would pardon with a good heart, and perhaps I could have done, if you had said nothing to anyone. I was silent myself, remember... why, why did you not follow my example? Why, why, unhappy one, reveal to all the secret of the punishment imposed on me by my mother? Alas, sweet friend, you have been so much to me and we could have lived the same, even when our love turned to hate, to distress, to hardness, to tears, to sadness. If you had not broken your word I could have remained in this world and been saved from torment and misery in the other. I could have lived out my life like a normal woman. I could have died quite naturally, ministered by the sacraments, and God would perhaps have received me into Paradise where we would have been reunited, one after the other, you, then our children later...

"On the contrary, I am now condemned to suffer bitter punishment until the Last Day of Judgment. To suffer without rest, nor truce, or hope of a provisional respite, until the end of time, without a tomb. For you have reduced me to miss my possible grave, though I ask for one on my knees, dream of it, weep for it, while knowing that my plaint on this subject, like all other, is useless. But the cruel thing, the cruellest thing is that all this came from you, from you alone!"

Unable to bear her immense distress, so resigned, with so little reproach, he was filled with an anguish so poignant that, almost fainting, he knelt before his wife as if in prayer, and raised his joined his hands toward her.

"My life, my good, my hope and my honour, in the name of the glorious suffering of Our Lord Jesus Christ, in the name of the glorious pardon that the true son of God gave to Mary Magdalene, I beg you, forgive my misdeed and continue to live with me. There are enough days to live and tenderly forgive and forget what has come about, so small compared to all the rest."

Without replying, Melusine regarded him, and from her reddened eyes great tears fell onto her breast. Most happy to see him return to her, most unhappy at the thought of such lost happiness, failing this time to faint. And they stayed thus, he, crying with great sobs, she weeping also, more quietly and slowly.

She finished by pulling away from this last embrace where their unhappiness was kept between themselves, their suffering together, their sadness reconciled.

"Oh my tender Love returned again to me. May God forgive the fault you have committed, so demented, so useless, to the eternal loss of our mutual repose! He may, who is almighty, who is all forgiveness, the true fount of mercy and pity. As for me, know that I have forgiven you with all my heart, since I am your lover, your wife, and your companion. But alas, as for my living with you, all has come to an end. God, this same God, does not permit it!"

She rose so they could the better hold each other once more in each other's arms, and so remained a long time as one, and kissed and cried. Never were so many tears shed. And the more that they held together, the more deeply their feelings ran, until without knowing, their arms fell slack and both fell senseless to the ground.

The ladies and maidens, knights and squires, touched to the quick in the face of such distress began to weep in their turn, not unmindful that their customary life was also about to end, and cried:

"Fortune! How can you be so hard as to part such true lovers! We lose today the most wise, most just, and best of women! The heavens do not make many such in this world. One could search many countries for many years before finding another like her!"

The two knew no more than their distress and, in their dreams while swooned on the cold stones, they sought, without finding, how to return as they had been. But there was too great a distance between their former happiness and that in which they now lived, and they forgot that each one had been the cause of that. He through his curiosity, she, without it being her fault, by her very nature. And he no doubt threw the fault on her, and she told herself that they would still be happy but for his cursed curiosity.

And the leech, who was a philosopher, as he should be in so serious a profession as his predecessor Hesnin la Panouze, felt that in this so impermeably solid world, two beings, although total Love had brought them together, perhaps through mutual blindness, perhaps no longer united them. They could not become again what they had been when they had begun. They were free of each other then, but were no longer, and could now only become more and more separated, even enemies. All that composed their coming together did not permit them any longer to be indifferent, and the less so the longer they had lived together. Thus a misunderstanding once begun could not end up on the side of Love, but accentuated itself, since each took sides one against the other, rather than returning to how things had been before with the aim of becoming one. Why was it that one persists at first, through bad times, locked in one's own being, one's sole being, instead of realising that these dark hours are one reason more to banish them, to give themselves again to each other, more than ever before, and for always.

Ladies and damsels, squires and knights lamented so much that they ended up forgetting the objects of their grief before their eyes, to dream about themselves and their own problems. Thus they wept between themselves without thinking any more of the two former lovers who lay at their feet.

Melusine came to her senses first.

She rose, turned toward her husband still lying there, and in a lost voice whispered to him what must be their fate.

"My sweet Friend, believe me, I can alas no more live with you because of the fault you have so grievously committed, even though I forgive you with all my heart, remember what I say to you again with all my soul. Alas! God does not permit me to stay, so I tell you once more it is impossible for me to do so. But listen well to what I tell you before these people – since it is a hard truth and it is needful that you learn it. After you, my Raymondin, no man will be able to hold this country in such peace as we have seen and as it is held at present. After you, your heirs will have much success, but also punishing affairs, and some will be deprived of their heritage as well as their honour, by folly or by crime. But while you live, dear friend, I will help you from afar with all my power in all your needs and problems. Do not chase Geoffroy away from you; he will be a valiant man. We have, on the other hand, two more children, Raimonnet the elder, who is only three years old, and Thierry, the younger, who is hardly two. Have them well brought up and looked after. Besides, I will watch over them myself, have no doubt about that. But you will never see me in the form of a woman again. It must be thus for our expiation to be complete."

Then standing apart with the highest barons she added in a muted voice:

"Good lords, hold to the honour of our union, of our name and our country. Promise me, as soon as I have gone, to put Horrible to death, that one of my sons who has three eyes, one of them in the forehead. Do not delay to carry out this important wish. For if you fail to do it, there will come much evil, misery, death and damage from him.

It was Raymondin who replied.

"My sweet Love, it will be done as you wish, since it appears that life is composed of dolorous necessities, to which we must submit! But, by the pity of God, do not drive me to death and dishonour! O Melusine, I pray you, stay! For if you do not I will never know joy in my heart again."

She began once more to cry.

"Who wants that more than I! But once more, remember, if that were possible, then believe me I would do it, with all my heart, with all my soul, with all my strength! What, in the world, could give me more pleasure than to be forever yours, in your arms, even – above all – to die? Alas! Alas! Alas! It cannot be. If you only knew – I feel a hundred times more the grief at our separation than you can ever feel yourself."

And, saying that, she kissed him hopelessly.

"Farewell, farewell, farewell, my Friend, my good, my heart, all my joy! So long as you live, I will have, even though absent from you, a single comfort. That of seeing you, to look over you and make you happy. But do not seek for that which cannot be. For I tell you once more, never again will you see me in the form of a woman. Farewell, farewell, half my soul! Farewell, half my heart! Farewell, half my life!

And suddenly, as if she were constrained to do it at that very moment, poor Melusine threw herself toward the window which looked out over the fields and gardens towards Lusignan – for do not forget they were at Marmande. She moved as easily and lightly as if she had wings. And even them she had soon, as all were to see.

Poised there – for it was good place to see – she took a last long look at the world below. Finally, turning to the one she loved:

"My beloved, here are two gold rings which have the same virtue. Keep them safe for the love of me. Whenever you wear them, neither you nor your heirs will be hurt in any battle as long as it in a just cause. Neither you nor they can be killed by any weapon if it is not the day of your destined death."

And he, who realised inexorable Fate, took them and kissed them, without saying more, except to himself.

Melusine looked out over the green meadows, and added in a voice so sad that everyone renewed their tears:

"Sweet and beautiful country, I must now leave you as well! I hope however to live until my end in loving you and admiring you, and being loved and admired by all myself... As for the present, those who see me will fear me as a venomous beast! Fate decrees it, and wills it to be thus. I must accept it, since there is no other!"

And she wept again at these last words.

"Farewell, farewell, each and every one of you. Pray devotedly to Our Lord to relieve my sufferings and shorten the time of my ordeal. Farewell my husband! Farewell my love! Farewell all loving! Farewell my all!"

Then tearing herself away, scratched and grazed by the frightful violence that she did to herself, she threw herself straight out of the window in the form of a winged serpent, about fifteen feet long. And there remained no more of her than the shape of her foot, imprinted in a small hollow on the window sill from which she had launched her rapid and despairing flight.

Afterword

André Lebey's version of the Romance of Melusine concludes a little before the description of her flying over the countryside of Poitou and occasional clandestine returning as reported by Jean d'Arras and Couldrette, authors of the original romance, in prose and verse respectively, in 1393 and 1401.

However, he includes the essentials of the original romance, and what he adds are evocative and detailed descriptions of high life in the middle ages. It may be a somewhat romantic and nostalgic pastiche as perceived through modern eyes but this is all to the good if it makes the story come alive for us. And this might not be the case if we had to rely only on a scholarly translation of the original texts. What is more, his modern psychological focus gives an added dimension to the main characters, of which the late 14th century authors would not have been capable.

We know that Jean d'Arras and Couldrette originally wrote to boost the claims of wealthy patrons, the Duke de Berry and the Lord of Parthenay respectively, who in the midst of the Hundred Years War had an interest in forwarding their real or imaginary connections to the castle of Lusignan. However, whatever the political motivation of their patrons, they built on genuine local faery traditions of the time.

There did already exist a legend of Melusine of Lusignan, as Pierre Bersuire (1285-1362) prior of the abbey of St. Eloi, had written about it at least a couple of generations before:

> They say that in my country the solid fortress of Lusignan was founded by a knight and a faery he married, and that the faery is the ancestor of a great number of noble and great persons, and the kings of Jerusalem and Cyprus, as well as the Counts of la Marche and Parthenay, are her descendents ... But the faery, they say, taken by surprise, naked, by her husband, transformed into a serpent. And today they still tell how when the castle changes master the serpent shows itself in the castle.
> *Reductorium morale.*

This is the general outline of the Melusine story and is also correct historically so far as it goes. For members of a cadet branch of the Lusignan family once ruled the crusader kingdoms of Jerusalem and Cyprus and members of the main family held the county of La Marche and lordship of Parthenay closer to home.

Jean d'Arras cites similar legends described by Gervaise of Tilbury (c.1152-1234) who some two hundred years before wrote a curious work in Latin called *Otia Imperialia* ("Diversions for Emperors").

> ... faeries take the form of very beautiful women, and various men have married them. They made them swear to various stipulations: some had to swear never to see them naked, others never to inquire into their actions on Saturdays, and still others never to try to see them during the lying in of childbirth. As long as they followed these stipulations, they enjoyed an elevated condition in life and great prosperity. But as soon as they betrayed their oaths, they lost their wives, and luck abandoned them little by little. And, of these beings, certain ones changed into serpents on one or several days during the week. That same Gervais says also that he believes it was because of some misdeeds unknown to the world which displeased God that He secretly punished them with these afflictions, such that none have knowledge of it but He.

And in particular he cites a legend given by Gervais, about:

> ... a knight named Roger du Castel de Rousset, in the province of Aix-en-Provence, who encountered a faery and wanted to take her as his wife. She agreed to it, on condition that he never seek to see her naked. They lived together for a long time, and the knight became more and more prosperous. It came about, then, that a long time afterwards, the said faery was bathing, and that he, out of curiosity, wanted to see her. But immediately the faery plunged her head under the water and changed into a serpent, never to be seen again.

If we are to take Gervais literally it must have been a pretty deep bath – possibly a well or natural pool of water – which suggests a connection to general faery lore and their association with natural springs and fountains. Many little fountains throughout France today have their plaster cast of the Virgin Mary or a minor saint who has taken over from the original faery spirit.

Jean d'Arras and Couldrette took great pains to emphasise Melusine's Christian credentials including being a good practising Catholic. This was no doubt with a view to neutralising the traditional ecclesiastical view about denizens of the Otherworld. In earlier times she would have been forthrightly condemned as a succubus demon.

This censorious attitude did gradually give way to a more liberal three fold vision. It was conceded that whilst all true miracles were of God and could only be performed by saints, and all magic and sorcery was of the Devil, there could also be a halfway house, of the marvellous, which had found its way into western culture through the vehicle of Celtic myth and legend in the Arthurian and Graal romances.

Even so, there was a tendency for romancers to hedge their bets by secularising the supernatural. In the romances of Chrétien de Troyes we find ladies with definite faery characteristics who, however, are not named as such, but passed off as ordinary human beings, as I have illustrated in *The Faery Gates of Avalon* (R.J. Stewart Books, 2008).

Laurence Harf-Lancner, in a doctoral thesis published as *Les Fées au Moyen Age,* makes some interesting points on the way faeries were referred to in romance literature. They were rarely named as such – but rather called ladies or maidens or lovers: (*pucelle, demoiselle, meschine, amie, dame, drue, la bele* rather than *fée* or *faé*). And there can also be a subtle distinction between *fée* (faery) and *faé* ("faeried") – the latter implying someone who is not completely faery, but may be a human under strong faery influence or with strong faery connections. Not that any writes with any great degree of consistency.

This raises the intriguing question, just how much of a faery was Melusine? The original romance gives her a human father and a faery mother, although we should perhaps not place great store on the accuracy of tales of her origins as understood in the 1390s. And a couple of recent French novels have tried to secularise her altogether [*Les dames de Lusignan* by Jarijo Chiché-Aubrun, Geste éditions 2006, and *La fée et le chevalier* by Jean-Marie Williamson, Editions des Deux Rives 2005] whilst Laurence Harf-Lancner considers faeries to be simply a 12th century literary invention.

This is an attempt at secularisation on a par with medieval attempts, albeit for different reasons. But faeries had been around a long long time in Brittany, Wales and Ireland before ever French courtly romancers realised they had the means of earning a good living off their backs.

So breaking out of the safe house of literary academe, and beyond the tangled psycho-analytical garden of archetypes of the unconscious, might it not be worth a shot at wandering or even questing into the wild woods of tradition to see if faeries might be beings in their own right? As tutelary spirits of individuals or families, or spirits of place, be it building or bosky grove – including the function of the traditional *bean sidhe* – who foretell impending changes to whatever or whomever they watch over. All of which Melusine was capable of being.

This is not too far a cry from traditional guardian angels, although they may have fallen into the modern secular discard too.

So indulging in a little metaphysical speculation, if we look for an Otherworld condition that is neither the celestial one of angels nor the hellish one of demons, we are pushed to a consideration of a lesser known aspect of Nature, the inner side of the Earth itself.

In Dante's great medieval poetic vision there is an intermediate condition known as the Earthly Paradise. Which is to say, in more modern language, an image of the Earth, outside of time, conceived as an ideal in the Universal Mind.

If there were such, any denizens of such an Otherworld might well pertain to what we can discern of the faery condition. Beings of great beauty, with certain extra-dimensional powers, and a penchant for perfection of form. On the down side of this there does appear to be a certain uncompromising element about them. For all its beauty there is an element of the faery world that can be cruel and unforgiving, perhaps the flip side of a penchant for static perfection.

Compared to this the human world we know is one of a messy, compromising struggle of give and take, ever in a state of change. In Biblical terms perhaps the result of tasting the fruits of the Tree of the Knowledge of Good and of Evil through the exercise of Free Will – which seems to sum up the human condition. In this respect, the expulsion from the Garden of Eden (the Earthly Paradise by another name), was in a sense a Fall "upwards". The way back may be long and painful and weary, but with it comes the capacity for grace and forgiveness, and possibly a final state higher than that of those who stayed behind – somewhat outside of space and time but holding the original vision of perfection, of an ideal world.

Be this as it may, do we find in the faery tradition a record of occasional attempts to cross the divide between the two parallel worlds?

Such an interchange can apparently be a two way transaction. For just as there are, like Melusine, cases of a faery attempting to enter the human world, so are there tales of a human entering the faery one. Harf-Lancner indeed finds a useful distinction in classifying faeries as either "Melusinian" or "Morganatic". That is to say, those who seek a human lover as a means to enter the human world, against those who take a human by force or seduction off to faeryland. There are also, as in Breton lais, intermediate cases.

The reasons for such rare attempts must remain speculative, but it is possible that individual and even collective good may come out of such experiments. But it can be a dangerous game with dire results if either side should get it wrong. Which is no more nor less than can be said of any form of exploration and discovery.

Anyhow, let us lower the barriers of disbelief to consider the options, for our own metaphysical speculation might well be a deal better than that of Jean d'Arras and Couldrette, who tend to regard Avalon as a pretty miserable kind of place and denizens of it in a state of poverty and despair.

With regard to the mechanics of things, elements of a faery approach would seem to summon the necessary power to cross the divide by means of erotic attraction – possibly aided by great psychological trauma in the beginning – as in the case of Raymondin or Hervé de Leon.

From this initial connection a fruitful interchange may then flow, but which must be based on continuing complete mutual trust and protected by confining walls of mutual secrecy. Raymondin's and Melusine's liaison could perhaps have survived the initial breach of trust between them, had he not broken all bounds by announcing their breach to the world. The dire result was thus not necessarily the consequence of an irrevocable maternal curse upheld by an unforgiving deity but simply a matter of metaphysical mechanics – akin to puncturing a hole in a space craft or a diving bell. When things are out of their natural element, then one has to be very cautious indeed about breaking the safety rules.

This seems pretty typical of most accounts of human/faery liaison. What we find unique in the Melusine story are the various defects in her sons. We do not know where Jean d'Arras got these ideas or details from or whether he simply made them up. It has been suggested that they show that an element of the animal or the wild may be a part of the faery condition. Possibly so. As drugs in pregnancy may induce abnormalities, or close familial relationship, so perhaps conceptions between the worlds have their risks. One or two of the marks, a lion's paw, or boar's tusk-like tooth, or furry patch on nose, are obvious – but there are also elements of compensation. Regnault, who has only one eye, has, in the original romance, sight that is far superior to any human optical powers in much the same way that members of the animal kingdom have senses superior to the human.

On the other hand, defects can go beyond minor blemishes of complexion or facial proportions, to a fierce and uncontrollable boar-like wildness with Geoffroy, or a complete bestiality with the grotesque Horrible whom even Melusine thinks should be put down in the common interest.

Is all this part of a general scheme whereby the gateway between Faery and Human worlds is perforce by way of the Natural or Animal world? There is an interesting tradition known as the Threefold Alliance that expresses the need for some kind of rapprochement between all three conditions of life – as developed by R.J. Stewart in *The Living World of Faery* (Gothic Image 1995).

As to Melusine's need to have a period of time to herself each week, it is possible that this is not necessarily the result of a curse but of the need for her to recharge her faery batteries, so to speak. She is a creature in an alien world who must have been under constant strain to maintain her appearance and function in an alien environment.

The chosen day is that of a traditional day of rest – the original Jewish Sabbath, although in other accounts the Christian Sunday is preferred.

There are elements within this and other tales that suggest that the revelation of the faery condition pertaining at such times is not one that the faery likes to be seen. One wonders why. Is it that the appearance would be grotesque to the human observer? In a sense it has a resonance with the tradition of the loathly damsel or the frog prince.

Much speculation has been given to the serpentine traditions of Melusine that go back to Celtic or Scythian serpent gods, there apparently having been a Scythian Roman legion based in Poitiers, but they seem to take the focus from the essentials. One might do better to take a more elemental approach and view the serpentine form of brooks and rivers that stem from springs.

At which point we may as well leave this line of intellectual metaphysical speculation to concentrate on simple imagery, which by the power of the imagination allied to belief can work greater wonders. That is to say, make the first steps on a real journey, rather than contemplate an atlas.

And what better way than to go once more through the Romance of Melusine as envisioned by André Lebey, who as a freemason would likely have known a great deal about the power of the visual imagination when invoked in certain directions, and thus writes with a greater validity than perhaps may be suspected! All we have to do is to allow the images to rise, and in his vivid treatment, he has met us more than half way if we care to contemplate his descriptions in an appropriately meditative frame of mind. To open the magic casements of vision.

CPSIA information can be obtained at www.ICGtesting.com
Printed in the USA
LVOW131903150313

324527LV00002B/388/P